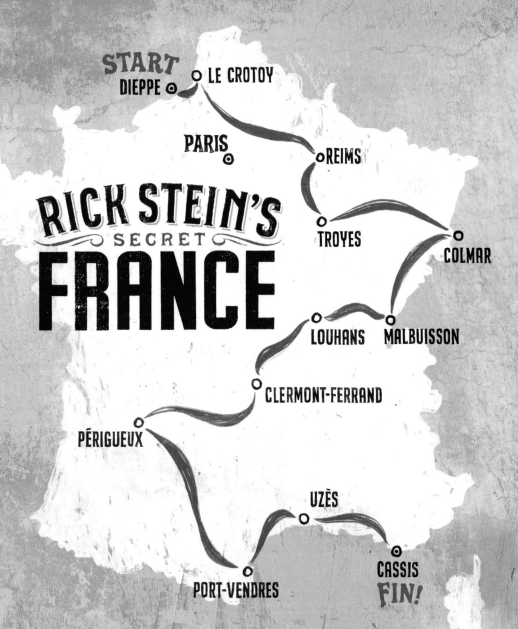

START
DIEPPE ⊙   ⊙ LE CROTOY

PARIS ⊙   ⊙ REIMS

RICK STEIN'S
SECRET
FRANCE

TROYES ⊙   ⊙ COLMAR

LOUHANS ⊙   ⊙ MALBUISSON

CLERMONT-FERRAND ⊙

PÉRIGUEUX ⊙

UZÈS ⊙

CASSIS
FIN!

PORT-VENDRES ⊙

RICK STEIN'S

SECRET

FRANCE

BBC
BOOKS

Pour vous servir
NOUS SOMMES
OUVERT
LUN 10H 18H
MAR 10H 19H
MER 10H 19H
JEU 10H 19H
VEN 10H 19H
SAM 10H 19H
DIM 10H 13H

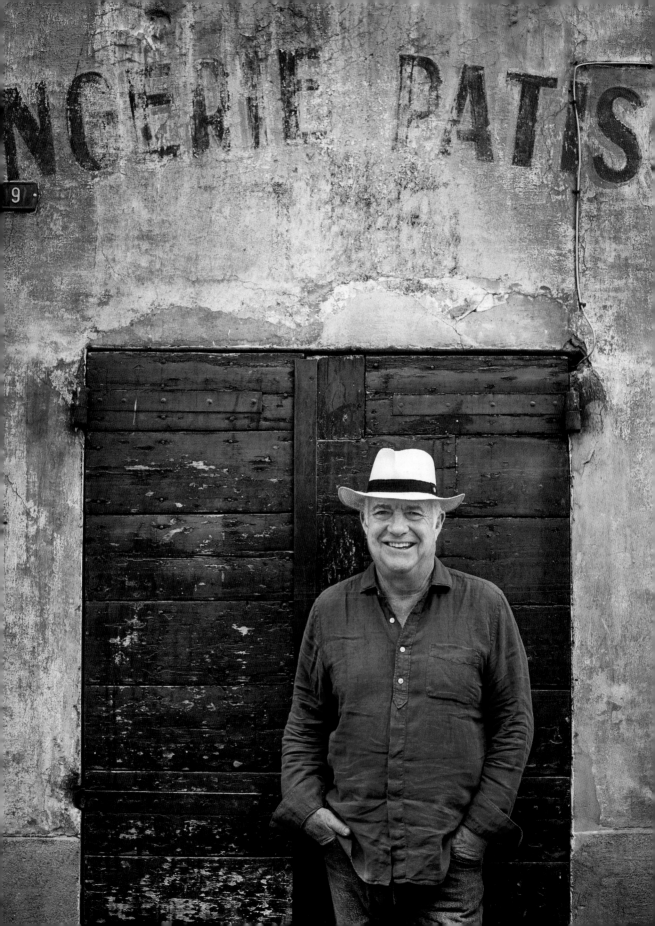

David Pritchard, my director, rang me a couple of years ago suggesting that we did a series in France, finding those sorts of places that meant so much to us when we were young. 'You're somewhere in the centre of La Belle France. You think, I'll just take a first left but I won't know where it leads; perhaps to a little winery that serves a bit of food or better still, a family-run restaurant with a no-choice menu using what was good at the market that morning. It's one of life's great pleasures to travel hopefully. Maybe waiting for you in a little auberge will be a steaming bowl of lentils and local sausages, with a fresh baguette and white butter.'

I could see myself motoring down long, straight roads bordered by plane trees with the sun flickering through and views of horses and deep grass or rows of vines with yellow sunlight everywhere, or passing through villages of honeyed stone with tiny tiles on the roofs, high and steep sloping. Somewhere, maybe in the Auvergne or Jura, I would find myself zigzagging up some frighteningly steep mountainside, still green but precipitous, nervously edging round each hairpin bend above a dizzying drop into some deep green valley with a river at the bottom and a red-roofed château almost hidden by trees.

Then my dreams became reality. I was waiting for a band to strike up in the square in Mauriac in Cantal, with a glass of Pelforth Blond in my hand. I'd never been to Mauriac before and I'd just been into the Romanesque church of Notre-Dame-des-Miracles and discovered the most heavenly of grotesques, a little old lion trying to look fierce, a many-coloured Romanesque baptismal font and a black Madonna of the miracles. The layers were so rich, and all the time I was thinking: this is my secret France.

Like many people, I have a romantic attachment to France that goes back to childhood, but when I was 16, a short stay near Cambrai in northern France converted me to the cuisine. The family, friends of my parents, owned a sugar beet farm of many hectares and also grew haricots verts and petits pois. They had servants and a butler who waited on my 11-year-old sister Henrietta and me at lunch and dinner. I should have realised even then that food would feature strongly in my life. I vividly remember a potato soup flecked with watercress and black pepper, and a fillet steak roasted whole, then thickly sliced and served rarer than rare *au jus* – not with a fancy sauce, simply the pan juices. The steak came with pommes frites, crisp and pale, and best of all – petits pois from the farm, not fresh but tinned. On another occasion we had a casserole of rabbit flavoured with curry powder (they kept rabbits, white ones, in cages); there were the biggest cherries I'd ever seen for dessert, and for me every day, the crowning glory: as much fizzy dry cider as I wanted, poured into my thick glass by the white-gloved butler.

My deep affection for France started then and has continued. I owe my love of food and restaurants to early trips to Brittany, getting off the ferry from Plymouth, in Roscoff and driving in spring through fields of artichokes to Le Conquet near Brest, a fishing village famous for its crabs. A cold clear breeze in April with a smell of seaweed on it and then a first plateau de fruits de mer – cockles, clams, mussels and oysters – all somehow repeating that fragrant coldness. I remember a plate of tiny scallops called pétoncles in the village of Plougastel. They were grilled in the shell with just a little salty Brittany butter left to go brown under the heat and then sprinkled with lemon juice and parsley. The produce was exquisite and the memory stays with me, not only because France was the first place where I really began to understand the enormous power of great produce and cooking to change my life, but also because I was in love with the country.

Perhaps, though, France, with memories like these, is just a state of mind. I think today we're living in nostalgic times because of so much rapid change and a sense that things were better in the past. Of course, we all know deep down that is rarely true; we were all just younger then and things felt better.

Nevertheless the idea that things are not as they once were with food in France prevails, not just in this country but in parts of the world influenced by French cooking, such as Australia, New Zealand and the USA. Would a latter-day Alice Walters and Jeremiah Tower, the driving forces of Chez Panisse in Berkeley, California, now be so inspired by youthful trips to France that they built a whole restaurant around the experience? I doubt it, partly because that's been done before now, but also these days many people believe that the food in France is just not as good. It's often remarked that the baguettes in the boulangerie are not what they used to be or that the menus in restaurants are so samey. I agree, there is a dreariness about so many menus: too many salades niçoise, salades au lard or salade au gésiers in the southwest. For mains, there's inevitably steak haché, magret de canard and lots of boeuf bourguignonnes and coq au vins. Too many restaurants are buying in finished dishes, which are made not at the local charcuterie or pâtisserie but in industrial estates. Such is the state of the restaurant industry and it's a welcome sight to see on a menu the words 'fait maison'.

It's understandable. The cost of labour is high. Many blame the 35-hour week and the fact that overtime has to paid for those working longer, but we are both first-world countries and we should be paying good wages. Few customers, however, are prepared to pay the price of producing simple French food made *au maison*. The consequence is that serving what I would call Michelin-style food is almost the only way to prosper. I should add that Michelin has no preferred style of cooking. It's just the way the guide is perceived.

When we filmed the previous series I made in France called *French Odyssey*, a trip from Bordeaux to Marseille on the canals of southern France, we took over the kitchen of a friend living near Agen so I could cook dishes that I'd picked up on the way. We stayed in a nearby restaurant with rooms; though the rooms were spartan the restaurant was magnificently overdecorated, as was the menu. The place didn't have Michelin stars but it aspired to, and the food was awful – needlessly complicated, elaborately described and very expensive. It was full at the weekends and I felt sorry for all those French people who thought of it as somewhere quite special.

I see this overpriced, over-elaborate food everywhere, absurdly delicate plates of little twists of chives, cubes of tomato, smears and foams. The received wisdom is that restaurants should produce dishes that you wouldn't cook at home, but I think back to the mid-70s and the first year my restaurant in Padstow opened, when a woman asked why she should pay 25p for new potatoes when she could cook them at home for nothing? Even then I thought, well, they are my potatoes from my sandy garden on Trevose Head, and I had scrubbed the skins off and cooked them with lots of salt and mint the way I like them. That's been my way of restaurant cooking ever since: buy the best and keep it simple is my secret if you like, and the secret I was looking for in France.

Perhaps part of the problem is that generally the French seem only to like their own food. There just isn't the variety of cuisines that you find in the UK. Even in larger towns they don't have Thai, Indian, Italian or Chinese restaurants, or Aussie- and Californian-influenced cafes. They don't have many foreign-themed chain restaurants either – other than McDonalds, of which there are many. There's just French, a few Vietnamese, North African and the odd Italian. I didn't go to any large city other than Marseille on this journey; things would certainly have been different in Paris or Bordeaux, but everywhere else it's all French. I remember something that a friend of mine said while dining just outside Saint-Rémy de Provence, 'The French like being French'. This is true. They want to keep their traditions, they want to close their kitchens after lunch at 2 o'clock; they want, as happened to me in Mauriac, to agree that yes, they do have a table for eight, but the chef says he doesn't want to cook for that many people at 9.00pm; it's too late.

But while I was making this journey I felt a mixture of frustration at being too late for lunch and admiration that they do still have a reassuring formality about mealtimes. I see it as a problem of our age that everything is becoming more informal and less structured, whether it be grammar, manners or religion. We welcome a relaxed approach to everything but there's a price to be paid and we all need boundaries. For this reason it's very satisfying for most of us, I would guess, to find a restaurant with rigid hours, a no-choice menu and a sense of timelessness, somewhere like Le Bistro du Paradou near Arles. Does anyone really care that there's only a no-choice menu there, I wonder? Or that it's always tête de veau with sauce ravigote on Tuesdays and chicken cooked on the rotisserie on Thursdays. Or that the only first course is vegetable soup?

I think not, if that soup is soupe au pistou and it's autumn, when the large steaming bowl contains freshly dried pulses like flageolets, as well as carrots, tomatoes, potatoes and green beans, all cut into thumbnail-sized pieces and imbued with the flavours of olive oil, garlic, Parmesan and basil. It was Thursday, so after the soup there was roast chicken and it just came with gravy. Dessert I don't remember, but there were seven of the best local cheeses, the wine was a Provence rosé, and the conversations were memorable.

I wrote to a friend of mine, Michael Aalders, who has a really good monthly blog about dining in France, telling him about the bistro. He replied with a photo of a just-finished empty plate with the knife and fork dropped on it, just like we do on our TV series, having finished something delicious – actually the TV crew having finished something delicious – with two words about the Bistro, 'Quite right'.

Yes, I know, you may ask what's so secret about Périgeaux, Dieppe, Troyes, Collioure, Marseille or Cassis, but the object of this book is to bring your attention to some of the best dishes in France, like one containing fabulous walnut oil from the Dordogne, and also to highlight things I discovered off the beaten track in places like Rochejean in the Haut-Jura, where I found a simple bilberry tart. I've had to modify the recipe to use blueberries because it's almost impossible to get bilberries in the UK, but Alpine bilberries are the taste of the mountains and trust me, to get to that restaurant you'll need to go seriously off the beaten track. Or in the village of Trizac in the Auvergne where the butcher and his wife make the most unlikely terrine called pounti, a curious mixture of pork, Swiss chard and prunes, which is very good as part of a lunchtime picnic of cooked meats, terrines, pâtés and salads.

This book is an account of a trip I've been lucky enough to make, meandering through the back roads of France, partly for nostalgic reasons and partly to answer the question 'Is French cuisine still alive and well?' With a few reservations I hope you'll see that yes, indeed it is, but more importantly there's plenty of evidence in the book that the cooks of the next generation are not standing still.

I finish with a little memory of a restaurant in Languedoc-Roussillon, which you might either love or hate but certainly you couldn't be indifferent about. Bar Biquet on Plage Mouret is right on the beach. It's built every spring, dismantled in late September, then reconstructed the following spring. The kitchens, store areas and toilets are made out of shipping containers and most of the restaurant consists of awnings and wooden boards laid on the beach. Biquet himself is a large, imposing man who is in love with bric-a-brac; the whole restaurant is kitted out in rusty chairs with ripped vinyl. It looks a bit like a job lot from a provincial airport circa 1963. There are mannequins wearing flying helmets and others of bare-breasted women with gas masks. The music is loud and on the night I was there the band was fabulous and so was the food. Biquet kindly offered me a look around the kitchen shipping container – actually it was more than one with the sides sawn off – and it was filled with very young chefs, both boys and girls, cooking up a storm. When people say cooking is the new rock and roll, this place lives up to that. The dishes came thick and fast: fried octopus with green tomato aïoli, burrata with heritage tomatoes and tapenade, pamboli (dried bread rubbed with garlic and tomato and drizzled with olive oil) with Palamos anchovies, bourride of monkfish and potatoes, and finally more octopus, this time slow-cooked and served with a rich beef stock and red wine sauce and pomme purée. Suddenly I thought, 'How cool. French cuisine is moving on'.

David Pritchard

David died earlier this year. He had been ill with cancer for some time, but *Secret France* was very much his inspiration. Sadly, he couldn't come away with me and the crew this time.

At 5.29pm he liked us all to be seated in a bar somewhere, having finished work for the day (the fact that it rarely happened didn't matter), just about to drink the first ice-cold beer, which as he would say, 'wouldn't touch the sides.' It's still the main reason we all love our trips, anticipating the first beer after work. It was David's boundless enthusiasm that captivated everyone, and not just for food but for everything and that to me was the reason he was such a great director. I miss him and wonder what filming will be like without him.

OEUFS ET FROMAGES

Quite near the town of Doubs in Franche-Comté there's a small village called Saint-Antoine, and a short drive through the Jura mountains is Fort Saint-Antoine, an old military fort of vaulted stone built into the hillside so all you can see is the front façade. It's been used to mature Comté cheese since the 1960s, when the affineur Marcel Petite realised that the most popular cheese in France could be successfully aged in the perfect cool and damp atmosphere of the fort. Today there are roughly 100,000 wheels of Comté being matured there at any one time and they stay there for up to two years.

While I was talking to Claude Querry, the chef de cave, and tasting the various maturities from the youngest to vieux Comté, I was thinking that the attention to detail happening here is the reason that French produce is so very good. The cheese is stored on wooden shelves many metres high and in endless aisles that you could easily get lost among. Robots trundle ceaselessly along them, sliding a cheese out, washing the rind with a weak salt solution, turning it and sliding it back. The shelves were made out of spruce wood and the reaction between the cheese and the wood is an important flavour element. Claude himself taps every cheese with a cheese iron called a sonde to check for density and possible hollows. At the other end of the sonde is a tiny borer that removes a 'carrot' from the cheese for tasting, and having sampled a tiny piece Claude returns the plug to the cheese and smooths it over. In the younger cheeses the sort of flavours he is looking for are such things as grass, hay, cauliflower or mushroom; in older cheeses, nuts, meat stock, pepper, coffee, dark chocolate or smoke.

Comté cheese is made at fruitières and the farms that supply these can be no more than 25km away, so each area has its own particular pastoral characteristics. Locally, the taste is always for the young cheeses, and I must say that in Arbois in the Jura I ate an omelette made with young Comté, accompanied by a glass of yellow Savagnin wine, that I think is the best I've tasted anywhere. In Franche-Comté, long-matured Comté cheese is regarded as a bit of a Parisian affectation – fromage de snob – but personally I think it's exquisite in its dry nuttiness.

This chapter contains generally rather rich and gorgeous French recipes featuring eggs, cheese and lots of butter. Indeed, a couple of them come from a restaurant in Haut-Jura at Malbuisson where I had an eight-course dinner of cheese. But go into any decent French restaurant in France and there will be that distinctive, overpowering smell of aged mature Époisse and Pont l'Évêque. Where else in the world is it completely acceptable to walk into a restaurant that's smelling a bit whiffy – don't you just love it? It's reassuring, and you know a nice glass of red will soon be on the way.

A croque monsieur should have an element of crispness to it since the French verb croquer is onomatopoeic, meaning to crunch or crack. For me, it means a crisp, toasted sourdough sandwich put together quickly with a little béchamel. The normal cheese and ham 'toastie' that's served up in motorway service stations as a croque monsieur I would simply class as a stomach filler. This, on the other hand, is a pleasure, from the crisp toast to the hint of bay leaf and nutmeg in the béchamel, and the Gruyère cheese and good ham inside.

CROQUE MONSIEUR

SERVES 2

10g butter, softened
    for spreading
4 slices sourdough bread
1–2 tsp Dijon mustard
85g Gruyère or Comté
    cheese, grated
2 thick slices good-quality
    ham (about 50g each)
A few rasps freshly
    grated nutmeg

Béchamel
25g butter
25g plain flour
270ml whole milk
1 bay leaf
A few rasps freshly
    grated nutmeg
Salt and black pepper

For the béchamel, melt the 25g of butter in a pan, then add the flour and stir for a couple of minutes. Take the pan off the heat and gradually whisk in the milk, beating after each addition to avoid lumps. Add the bay leaf, put the pan back on the heat and bring to the boil, then cook, stirring all the time, until thickened. Season with nutmeg, salt and pepper, then set aside.

Preheat the grill to a high setting. Butter the slices of bread on one side and place them buttered-side up under the grill until golden. Preheat the oven to 220°C/Fan 200°C.

Spread the untoasted sides of the bread with Dijon mustard. Spread 2 of the slices with some of the béchamel, then add a quarter of the grated cheese and a slice of ham to each one. Top with the remaining slices of toast, toasted side up, and spread with the remaining béchamel sauce. Sprinkle over the rest of the cheese and season with nutmeg and black pepper.

Transfer the sandwiches to a baking sheet and bake them for 10–12 minutes until golden and bubbling. Eat at once!

The etiquette of the dinner party now is such that not only can you not call it a dinner party – it's 'coming round for a meal' – but also you can't be seen to be putting any effort into the first course. If, though, you can carry off something incredibly simple and casual, everyone still loves a starter. This is just that. All you do is layer up slices of goats' cheese in ramekins, add seasoned crème fraiche, sprinkle with chopped walnuts and bake. The tartness of the cheese and crème fraiche served with crisp apple slices is a fabulous combination. It's the sort of thing that would be nice to find in a bar late morning somewhere in Paris to enjoy with a coffee or a glass of wine.

WARM GOATS' CHEESE WITH CREAM & WALNUTS

CHÈVRE CHAUD À LA CRÈME

SERVES 4
as a starter

15g butter, for greasing
200g young goats' cheese
  log, cut into 12 slices
200g full-fat crème fraiche
15g walnuts, chopped
1 tsp chopped flatleaf parsley
Salt and black pepper

To serve
2 apples, cored
  and finely sliced
Slices of crusty bread

Preheat the oven to 200°C/Fan 180°C.

Butter 4 ramekins, then put 3 slices of goats' cheese in each one. Season the crème fraiche with half a teaspoon of salt and plenty of black pepper and pour it over the cheese, dividing it equally between the ramekins.

Top with more black pepper and chopped walnuts, then bake for 15–20 minutes. Garnish with parsley and serve with slices of crisp apple and good bread.

I'm much taken with ordering cheese, rather than dessert, in a restaurant, particularly if, as is often the case, I've had fish with a glass of white Burgundy. Cheese gives me a perfect excuse to finish with a glass of red, something simple such as a Côtes du Rhône. I've always loved the French combination of walnuts, honey, fruit and a characterful cheese. This dish also makes a nice light starter.

QUARTERED FIGS WITH SOFT GOATS' CHEESE & HONEY

SERVES 4

8 figs, quartered
150g soft goats' cheese
4 tbsp runny honey
Small handful of
  walnuts or hazelnuts
  roughly chopped
Black pepper

Divide the figs and cheese between 4 plates. Drizzle with honey and sprinkle with nuts, then season with black pepper.

Somewhere in this book I had to include a tartine, for me the most perfect snack. It's got to be made with sourdough bread drizzled with olive oil and toasted, and this recipe is pretty much the classic. I firmly believe that in all dishes with raw tomato the tomato must be separately seasoned with salt and black pepper. *Recipe photograph overleaf.*

OPEN SOURDOUGH SANDWICH
UZÈS TARTINE

SERVES 2

2 slices sourdough bread
3 tbsp olive oil
1 clove garlic, grated
2 tomatoes, sliced
2 tbsp Green pistou
   (page 302)
75g goats' cheese
   log, sliced
2 tbsp Sundried tomato
   pistou (page 302)
A few basil leaves
Salt and black pepper

Preheat the oven to 200°C/Fan 180°C. Place the slices of sourdough on a baking tray and drizzle over 2 tablespoons of the olive oil.

Mix the remaining oil with the grated garlic. Put the tomato slices in a bowl, add the garlic and oil, then season with salt and pepper and turn until all the slices are coated. Arrange them on a separate baking tray. Place both baking trays in the oven for about 10 minutes.

Spread the slices of toast with the green pistou, then layer on the slices of tomato and goats' cheese. Top with the sundried tomato pistou and basil leaves, then sprinkle with a little more salt and pepper.

This is a speciality of Nice and is filled with Niçoise salad ingredients. Pan bagnat (sometimes pan bahnat) is the Niçard/Nissart dialect name – pan is their word for pain (bread). Originally a great way to use up slightly stale bread, the recipe contains tuna and anchovies, but if you're vegetarian you could substitute cheese (maybe mozzarella or slices of goats' cheese) or roasted peppers, aubergines, courgettes and mushrooms. Make this a day ahead and keep it weighted down in the fridge so all the juices seep into the bread. Perfect picnic food.

PROVENÇAL PICNIC SANDWICH

PAN BAGNAT

SERVES 6-8

1 pain de campagne or
    round sourdough loaf
    (about 400g)
1 clove garlic, finely
    chopped or grated
3 tbsp extra virgin olive oil
1 small red onion, finely sliced
2 or 3 large ripe tomatoes,
    sliced
15cm piece of cucumber,
    sliced
225g tuna in olive oil,
    drained
6 anchovies in olive oil,
    drained
3 hard-boiled eggs,
    peeled and sliced
20 Niçoise or Kalamata
    olives, pitted and halved
1 tsp oregano or marjoram
    leaves, chopped
10 basil leaves, torn
1 handful rocket leaves
1 tbsp red wine vinegar
1 tsp Dijon mustard
Salt and black pepper

Slice off the top quarter of the loaf to use as a lid. Using your fingers, hollow out the inside of the rest of the bread to leave just a shell.

Sprinkle the inside of the bread shell and the lid with the garlic, then brush with 2 tablespoons of the olive oil.

Layer in the vegetables, tuna, anchovies, eggs, olives, herbs and rocket, seasoning with salt and pepper as you go; the order doesn't really matter. Mix the remaining olive oil with the vinegar and mustard, then drizzle in this dressing so it trickles down over the filling.

Top with the bread lid and wrap the loaf tightly in foil. Place it in a baking tin and weigh it down with a heavy pan, a four-pack of tinned tomatoes or similar, then leave it in the fridge overnight. Serve cut into wedges.

I have no objection to truffle oil, indeed I like it, but let's make no mistake: it's not made from truffles. This is a view shared by Edouard Aynaud who has been harvesting truffles on his farm near Saint-Cyprien in the Périgord for many years. He's also been involved in exporting Mediterranean oak trees with truffle spores attached to places all over the world, notably to Australia and New Zealand where black truffles are being grown successfully. Cheapest are summer truffles, which have a black skin and grey interior and are picked in the summer. They have a good, slightly crunchy texture but very little flavour. Black truffles are black all the way through when ripe, although off-white when not. They're very expensive, common to Périgord and the South of France generally and harvested in autumn and winter. They have an intense earthy fragrance with some sort of pheromone quality to it that's curiously satisfying, though maybe less so when Edouard tells you that the reason that they used to use female pigs to find truffles was that they were attracted to the male pheromone scent of a truffle. These days, dogs are the norm, in Edouard's case his delightful collie Lino, but dogs want to eat the truffles so you have to have a pocketful of treats to distract them. Finally, white truffles only occur in the Piedmont region of Italy and Croatia. They are absurdly expensive, but a couple of slices can transform an egg dish like my brouillade. However, if you infuse whole eggs for a day or so with black truffle the flavour develops in a remarkable way. *Recipe photograph overleaf.*

BLACK TRUFFLE & SCRAMBLED EGGS

BROUILLADE

SERVES 2

5 eggs (Burford browns
   give a great colour)
10g fresh black truffle,
   washed and dried
30g unsalted butter,
   at room temperature
2 tbsp double cream
2 slices good-quality bread,
   toasted and buttered
Salt and black pepper

Put the whole eggs (still in their shells) in a bowl with the truffle and cover with cling film. Refrigerate for 24 hours to allow the eggs to absorb the perfume of the truffle.

Slice the truffle thinly on a truffle slicer, or mandolin, or grate it. Crack the eggs into a bowl, beat them lightly with a fork and season with salt and plenty of pepper.

Melt the butter in a non-stick frying pan over a medium heat. Add the eggs to the pan and slowly break them up with a wooden spoon. Cook for a few minutes until the eggs are starting to set but are still creamy and soft, then stir in the double cream. Serve with the sliced or grated truffle on top and some hot buttered toast.

I was keen to gather as many simple, classic recipes as possible for this book, so a cheese soufflé had to be included. Emmental is the cheese normally associated with soufflés but, much as I love it with lots of unsalted butter and fresh baguette, I find it doesn't quite have the definite flavour needed for a soufflé. Partnered with crab meat, though, it's perfect. Soufflés aren't particularly difficult to make – they're basically a thick white sauce lightened with whisked egg white. The most important thing is to rush them to the table before they start to collapse. There's no point in trying to cook your soufflés longer or give them more structure, as they would then lack the exquisite ephemeral nature that makes them so loved. Next time you're thinking how wonderful Italian food is, remember the French soufflé.

CRAB & EMMENTAL SOUFFLÉ

SERVES 4–6
(depending on the size
of the ramekins used)

30g butter, plus 10g
    for greasing
30g plain flour
285ml whole milk
75g Emmental cheese,
    finely grated
100g white crab meat
30g brown crab meat
¼ tsp Dijon mustard
5 chives, finely chopped
2 eggs, separated, plus
    an extra egg white
Salt and black pepper

Preheat the oven to 200°C/Fan 180°C and put a baking sheet in the oven to heat up.

Butter the ramekins – 4 if fairly large, 6 if smaller. Melt the butter in a pan, then add the flour and cook for a couple of minutes. Take the pan off the heat and gradually whisk in the milk, beating after each addition to avoid lumps. Put the pan back on the heat and bring the sauce to the boil, then cook, stirring all the time, until thickened. Take the pan off the heat again and stir in the grated cheese, white and brown crab meat, mustard, chives, egg yolks, salt and pepper. Taste and add a little more salt if required. The sauce should be quite flavourful, as the egg whites will dilute the taste a little.

In a separate clean bowl, whisk the egg whites to soft peaks. Add a spoonful of the egg whites to the pan and stir it in to loosen the mixture, then carefully fold in the remaining egg whites with a large metal spoon. Scoop the mixture into the ramekins, then run your finger round the top of each one to help it rise.

Immediately transfer the ramekins to the hot baking sheet in the oven and bake for 16–20 minutes until the soufflés are golden and well risen. Serve immediately, with some buttered toast if you like.

If you're not too daunted when entering the North African sector of Marseille and are fascinated by all the little food stalls, and possibly also by the amount of drug deals going on all around you, you might want to know what to order so that you don't look like a completely green tourist. May I suggest a brik? It's a crisp, thin, filo-like pastry that normally encases a fried egg and lots of lovely cheese. I always find that the moment of slight panic I might feel when walking through a challenging part of a city can be much dispelled by good food. The reasoning is quite simple – if the people are producing dishes like this, they must be nice.

EGG, CHEESE & POTATO BRIK

SERVES 4

500g Maris Piper
    potatoes or similar
130g ricotta, curd cheese
    or soft goats' cheese
2 spring onions, thinly
    sliced on the diagonal
Small handful coriander,
    chopped
4 round sheets brik pastry
    (see suppliers, page 309)
    or 4 sheets filo pastry
1–2 tbsp harissa paste
4 eggs
1 egg yolk
About 500ml vegetable oil
Salt and black pepper

Chop the potatoes quite small and boil them in salted water until tender. Drain and crush them with the back of a wooden spoon, then allow to cool slightly.

Mix the potatoes with the cheese and spring onions. Season with salt, pepper and the chopped coriander.

Spread the surface of each round of pastry with harissa paste. On one half of a pastry disc, make a 'nest' with a quarter of the potato mixture, then break an egg into the nest and fold over the other half of the pastry. Brush the edges with egg yolk to seal. Repeat to make the remaining parcels. (If using filo pastry, very lightly brush the sheets with oil and fold in half. Assemble the filling as above, but then fold in the sides and roll very carefully to encase the filling. Seal the edges with egg yolk.)

Heat the oil to 175°C in a frying pan. Gently lower in the parcels, one or two at a time and cook for about 3 minutes, then carefully turn them over and repeat until golden and crisp. Transfer them to a plate lined with kitchen paper to absorb any excess oil and keep them warm while you cook the rest. Serve immediately while they're hot and crisp, with some green salad on the side.

Many versions of this leek tart or pie from Picardy exist, some with a top of puff pastry or brioche or with added ingredients like cheese or lardons. Being something of a purist I prefer just a case of really short shortcrust pastry, my mother's recipe, with plenty of leeks sweated down in butter, then bound with an egg and cream mixture and baked. Delicious.

LEEK TART FROM PICARDY

FLAMICHE

SERVES 6

Shortcrust pastry
200g plain white flour,
    plus extra for rolling
½ tsp salt
60g cold unsalted
    butter, cubed
40g cold lard or vegetable
    shortening, cubed
2 tbsp ice-cold water

Filling
75g butter
1.25kg leeks, cut in half
    lengthways, washed
    and cut into 1cm slices
300g full-fat crème fraiche
2 large eggs, lightly beaten
A few rasps freshly
    grated nutmeg
Salt and black pepper

First make the pastry. Put the flour, salt, butter and lard in a food processor and process until the mixture resembles fine breadcrumbs. Transfer it to a bowl and add enough of the water to make a smooth but not sticky dough.

Put the dough on a floured work surface and roll it out to a circle about 28cm in diameter. Place the pastry in a 25cm loose-bottomed fluted tart tin, then trim the edges and prick the base with a fork. Cover with cling film and refrigerate or freeze for at least 30 minutes.

For the filling, melt the butter in a large shallow pan, add the leeks and leave them to sweat, uncovered, over a medium to low heat for 20–30 minutes until soft, stirring occasionally. If the leeks seem very watery after this time, cook until the liquid has reduced. Stir in the crème fraiche and beaten eggs, then season well with salt, pepper and nutmeg.

Preheat the oven to 200°C/Fan 180°C. Remove the pastry case from the fridge or freezer, line it with baking parchment and fill with baking beans. Bake it for about 10 minutes, then remove the paper and beans and continue to cook for another 4–5 minutes to allow the pastry base to dry out a little. Turn the oven down to 190°C/Fan 170°C.

Fill the pastry case with the leek mixture and season with a little black pepper. Bake the tart for 25–30 minutes, then serve warm or at room temperature.

Anybody who can remember the 1960s and 70s will look back with affection to fondue evenings. As far as I can remember, steak in hot oil was more popular than cheese fondue, which only came with bread to dip, so I very much enjoyed having so many other dipping ingredients on my recent trip to Jura. There was ham, warm potatoes and cornichons, but they also serve it with mushrooms or slices of apple or pear. I tried using 100 per cent Comté cheese and 50/50 Comté and Emmental. Both were excellent – the Emmental slightly more stringy. Have a look in your garage. Any fondue sets still lingering there?

FRENCH FONDUE

SERVES 4

1 clove garlic, smashed
300ml dry white wine
    (preferably from Jura)
2 tbsp cornflour
500g Comté cheese or
    250g Comté and 250g
    Emmental, grated
Freshly ground black pepper
A few rasps freshly grated
    nutmeg (optional)

To serve
1 baguette, cut
    into 2cm cubes
400g new potatoes,
    boiled in their skins,
    cooled and halved
Any combination of
    apples or pears, cored
    and cut into cubes,
    figs cut into quarters,
    cubed ham, cornichons,
    button mushrooms

Rub the inside of the fondue pot with the garlic. Add the white wine to the pot and heat to simmering point. If you are not sure your fondue pan is suitable to use on the hob, use a saucepan and once the mixture is ready, tip it into the fondue pot.

Mix the cornflour with the grated cheese. Add the cheese to the wine, a handful at a time, stirring after each addition until melted and smooth. Do not allow the mixture to boil. Season with freshly ground black pepper and nutmeg, if using, and take the pot to the table. Adjust the heat under the pot to keep it warm without burning the base.

Serve with cubes of crusty bread, potatoes and accompaniments of your choice to dip in, and a crisp green side salad.

If you love pancakes stuffed with mushrooms, cheese and ham, ficelle picarde is going to be your dream come true. The dish comes from Picardy, and Cyril Carnel, the policeman husband of Cathy, our British guide in the Somme, made it for us at their home in the village of Auchonvillers, known incidentally to the troops in the First World War as 'ocean bloody villas'. Anyone who's been to the battlefields of the Somme will have noticed that all the villages around there are attractive and built in red brick in the same early 20th-century style. But the overall effect of the region is slightly sombre, bearing in mind that these houses were built to replace so many demolished by bombing and shelling. It's very moving.

CYRIL'S FICELLE, SAVOURY BAKED PANCAKES
FICELLE PICARDE

SERVES 4

Crêpes
120g plain flour
Large pinch of salt
1 egg, beaten with
    1 extra yolk
275ml whole milk
1 tbsp rapeseed oil

Béchamel
60g butter
40g plain flour
570ml whole milk
1 bay leaf
A few rasps freshly
    grated nutmeg
Salt and black pepper

Mushroom filling
30g butter, plus extra
    for greasing
2 banana shallots,
    finely chopped
1 bay leaf
3-4 fresh thyme sprigs
500g Portobello mushrooms,
    wiped and finely chopped
8 slices good-quality
    baked ham

To finish
100ml double cream
75g Gruyère cheese, grated

Sift the flour and salt into a bowl. Make a well in the centre, add the egg and yolk, then whisk in the milk a little at a time to make a smooth batter. Cover and leave to stand for about 30 minutes.

Wipe a non-stick frying pan over with oil. Pour in an eighth of the batter and swirl the pan to coat the base, then cook over a medium-high heat for about a minute. Flip the crêpe over and cook for a further minute. Slide it on to a warmed plate, then cover with a tea towel and repeat until you have 8 crêpes.

For the béchamel, melt the butter in a pan, then add the flour and stir for a couple of minutes. Take the pan off the heat and gradually whisk in the milk, beating after each addition to avoid lumps. Add the bay leaf, put the pan back on the heat and bring to the boil, then cook, stirring all the time, until thickened. Season with nutmeg, salt and pepper. Cover with a sheet of greaseproof paper to use to prevent a skin from forming.

For the filling, melt the 30g of butter in a frying pan. When hot and foaming, add the shallots and allow them to soften for a few minutes before adding the herbs and mushrooms. Stir to coat them in butter and cook until the moisture from the mushrooms has evaporated and the mixture is fairly dry. Season well.

Preheat the oven to 200°C/Fan 180°C. To fill the crêpes, place one on a board and add 2 tablespoons of béchamel and a slice of ham, then top with an eighth of the mushroom mixture. Fold in the ends of the crêpe and roll it up. Repeat to fill the rest. Butter an oven dish large enough to accommodate all 8 and lay them over the base. Pour over the remaining béchamel to cover them generously, then add the cream. Finally, sprinkle the grated cheese on top and season with more salt and pepper. Bake for about 20 minutes until golden brown and bubbling.

You might think that buckwheat galettes are native to Brittany and Normandy, but the inhabitants of the Auvergne would also claim ownership. This recipe comes from the town of Salers, famous for its cheese which is similar to Cantal but made only from the milk of cows grazing on mountain pastures in the summer. The town itself is extraordinary. As I've said elsewhere, no part of France is really that secret, but when I arrived in Salers on a sunny morning last June it felt like I'd just landed somewhere in Ruritania. There didn't seem to be a house in the central square that hadn't been transformed into some sort of castle by the addition of round towers or turrets. For lunch, we all ordered these hearty, yeasted pancakes. Exceptionally good though they were, none of us could finish them, so I've slightly reduced the amount of the delicious cheese that's part of any savoury dish in the area.

BUCKWHEAT PANCAKES WITH MUSHROOMS & EGGS

BOURRIOLS AUX CHAMPIGNONS ET À L'OEUF

SERVES 4

Batter
90g buckwheat flour
90g plain flour
½ tsp salt
6g fast-action dried yeast
1 large egg
325ml whole milk
225ml warm water
Rapeseed oil,
   for greasing

Filling
4 large flat mushrooms,
   wiped and sliced
2–3 tsp butter or olive oil
150–200g Cantal, Comté
   or Gruyère cheese,
   finely grated
4 eggs
A few flatleaf parsley sprigs,
   roughly chopped
Black pepper

Begin by making the batter. Pour the buckwheat and plain flours into a bowl and add the salt and dried yeast. Make a well in the centre, break in the egg and whisk it into the flour. Then whisk in the milk and warm water to make a smooth batter. Cover and leave in a warm place to allow the batter to rise for an hour or so – it should be frothy and sweet-smelling.

Fry the mushrooms in the butter or olive oil until tender, then set aside. Heat a 26–28cm non-stick frying pan and wipe it with a little oil. Stir the batter to make sure it is well combined.

Pour in enough of the batter to coat the base of the pan and cook the pancake over a medium-high heat for 2–3 minutes until it's golden brown and easily releases from the pan. Flip the pancake over – be careful, as these can be fragile. Break an egg into the centre of the pancake, then surround it with a quarter of the cheese. Cook until the white has set and then create a square by folding in the edges of the circle, leaving the centre open. Scatter some of the mushrooms over the egg and cheese.

Slide the pancake on to a large baking sheet and keep it warm in a low oven while you make the rest in the same way. Season the pancakes with plenty of black pepper and sprinkle with parsley, then serve with a soft green salad or wilted spinach.

The Auvergne was one of my favourite parts of the recent journey I made for this book. As I've said, I've called the book *Secret France*, even though I run the risk of people asking 'What's so secret about Dieppe, Burgundy or Cassis?' I do think, though, that the Auvergne is not much visited by the British, and I was thrilled to find a restaurant converted from an old garage in Trizac, a beautiful village lost in time. Dominique Peythieu, the woman who owns the restaurant, explained simply that when she inherited her father's mechanics workshop she turned it into a restaurant – not being a dab hand with a spanner herself. She cooked two dishes for me. First, this pachade, which is simply an Auvergnate pancake stuffed with cheese and ham, and second the sublime Agen prune tart on page 286. The cheese in her pachade was the local young Cantal and the meat an unsmoked dry-cured ham. I remember the lovely salty crisp exterior of this pancake, with its centre all puffed up and oozing cheese and ham.

SAVOURY AUVERGNE PANCAKE
PACHADE

SERVES 2

20g Parma ham
40g Cantal cheese
    (or good-quality mild
    or medium Cheddar)
4 tbsp plain flour
2 eggs
250ml whole milk
2 tsp vegetable oil
Salt and black pepper

Cut the ham and cheese into strips about 5mm thick. Put the flour in a bowl and whisk in some salt and pepper. Make a well in the centre and add the eggs, then whisk to make a thick batter. Add the milk to thin the batter to the consistency of double cream.

Heat the oil in a small non-stick frying pan (about 24cm in diameter) and place it over a high heat. Pour in the batter, it should puff up on contact. Leave it for a couple of minutes, then lay the slices of cheese and ham on top of the pancake. Cook it over a medium heat for a couple of minutes, then flip it over and cook for another minute or so on the other side. Cut the pancake in half and serve with a lightly dressed green salad.

Elizabeth David's short pieces are still some of my favourite food writing, Her, M. F. K. Fisher and a couple of others, such as Richard Olney and Brillat-Savarin, have the ability to link food, art and life in the subtlest of ways which is actually why I'd like to do a book on Japanese cooking one day. The title piece in David's book *Omelette and a Glass of Wine* seems to me to explain exactly what simple French cooking is all about. When Annette Poulard, proprietress of a restaurant in Normandy and celebrated for her omelettes, was asked why her omelettes were so wonderful, she replied: 'Here is the recipe for the omelette: I break some good eggs in a bowl, I beat them well, I put a good piece of butter in the pan, I throw the eggs into it, and I shake it constantly. I am happy, Monsieur, if this recipe pleases you.' Second only to a plain omelette, in my estimation the very best of French cooking, is an omelette aux fines herbes with parsley, tarragon, chervil and chives, all very finely chopped.

OMELETTE AUX FINES HERBES

MAKES 1

3 eggs
Small handful of mixed
   herbs: flatleaf parsley,
   tarragon, chervil and
   chives, chopped
1 tbsp butter
Salt and black pepper

Break the eggs into a bowl and beat them lightly with a fork. Add the chopped herbs and season with salt and pepper.

Melt the butter in a 25cm non-stick frying pan and swirl it around until foamy but not browned. Add the egg mixture and allow it to sit for 30 seconds, then using a wooden spatula or spoon, agitate the bottom of the pan as the eggs start to cook. Cook for 1–2 minutes allowing the eggs to set slightly. The surface should remain soft and creamy.

Tilt the pan and flip the top half of the omelette over the bottom half, then roll it out on to a warmed plate. Serve with a dressed green salad.

I do believe that the great French wines are best served with simple dishes. This white version of the classic red oeufs en meurette is incredibly easy to make and it's the perfect accompaniment to a serious glass of Saint-Romain Auxey-Duresses or Meursault. I know this because I spent an afternoon with Eric Bonnetain at Auxey-Duresses and afterwards Eric's son-in-law, Tom Kevill-Davies, cooked this dish and gave me a glass of the family's Auxey to drink with it. There is something about cream and white wine sauces that make a white Burgundy come alive. An egg like a Burford Brown with a really orange yolk makes this dish extra special.

EGGS IN A WHITE WINE SAUCE

OEUFS EN MEURETTE

SERVES 2

1 tsp white wine vinegar
2 fresh eggs (Burford
    Browns are good)
1 shallot, finely chopped
45g cold butter,
    cut into 2cm dice
100ml white wine
100ml Chicken stock
    (page 301)
1 thyme sprig
85ml double cream
2 slices Parma ham, grilled
    until crisp (optional)
A few chives, snipped
Salt and black pepper

Bring a pan of water to a simmer and add the vinegar. Crack an egg into a cup. Stir the water to create a whirlpool, then gently add the egg to the water. Cook for about 3 minutes. Carefully remove the egg with a slotted spoon and place it in a bowl of cold water. Repeat with the other egg and set them aside.

Add the shallot and 10g of the butter to a small frying pan. Cook the shallot over a low heat until translucent, then add the wine, stock and thyme and cook until the liquid is reduced by half. Pass through a fine sieve over a bowl, pressing the contents with a wooden spoon to extract as much flavour as possible, and discard the shallot and thyme. Tip the liquid back into the pan, then add the cream and bring to the boil. Turn the heat down to a simmer and whisk in the butter a cube at a time. Season with salt and pepper. Grill the slices of ham, if using, until crisp.

Before serving drain the cold water from the eggs and pour boiling water into the bowl. Leave for 45 seconds for the eggs to warm through.

Place each egg in a shallow soup bowl and pour over the sauce. Garnish with black pepper and chopped chives and add a crisp slice of ham, if using. Eat at once.

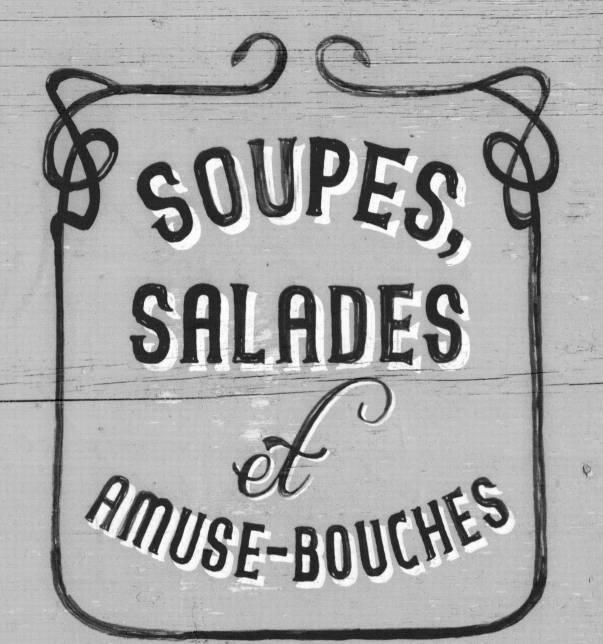

SOUPES, SALADES et AMUSE-BOUCHES

Apart from 'French restaurants aren't what they used to be' the other comment that people often make to me is 'Where do all the lovely vegetables and fruit in French markets go? They don't very often turn up on a menu.' I don't know whether in my travels I have successfully answered the question. What I have done is to continue my endless enthusiasm for the markets that take place once or twice weekly in the centre of beautiful French towns like Périgueux, Uzès or Louhans in Saône-et-Loire.

I can think of no better experience of the glories of French produce than the Wednesday or Saturday autumn marché in the town of Périgueux in the Dordogne. It's no coincidence that the photo on the front of this book is of me in front of a stall called La Férme Périgordine. In no way do I want to make adverse comparisons between French and British weekly markets, because farmers' markets in this country have come on in leaps and bounds, but the layers of expertise in France, both in the knowledge of those producing, whether it be plums, peaches, courgettes, tomatoes, garlic, onions or fabulous cheeses, pâtés, terrines and the freshest of fish, and the discernment of the customers buying, is one of the reasons that people love France so much.

But as I keep saying, the salads that you get in restaurants in France are often disappointing, so this chapter is my attempt to do justice to the immense diversity and attraction of the produce in French markets. And there are not only salads, but also some soup recipes and a few appetisers, the sort of things you might offer your guests when they arrive.

But it is not just French markets where such great produce abounds. Every year in June I stay just outside Ramatuelle near St Tropez. We mostly shop at the local Spar, which in addition to having a complete cornucopia of fruit and veg has as good a fish counter as you could ask for anywhere, with large sea bass, monkfish tails, weaver fish and plenty of mussels and clams, including praires and palourdes. There's also a fabulous butchers' counter with the best aged côte de boeuf and the lovely trussed joints of beef, lamb or pork so special to France. This Spar shop even sells poulet de Bresse, expensive but so worth the money, as well as perfectly trimmed beautifully trimmed carré d'agneau.

Being British I can't stop thinking – all this, in a SPAR shop! The friendly corner shop of our own country is a little different in France but the point is that it's much easier to eat well in France from local shops.

One of the rather pathetic realities of the fact that so many of the restaurants in France are disappointing these days is the almost tearful joy in finding one that's everything you would have hoped for, often from your childhood or teenage memories. Such a place is Le Bistro du Paradou near Arles. I've mentioned the restaurant and this soup in the introduction to the book, and like all great dishes it takes me back to the evening I ate it. I remember the large green tureen it was served in and the wonderful scent of basil, olive oil and garlic. I also recall the animated chat round the table with my friend John Illsley, his wife Steph and my wife Sas about the French and about the realities of his band Dire Straits writing 'Sultans of Swing' in a council flat in Deptford.

AUTUMNAL VEGETABLE SOUP WITH BASIL, GARLIC & OLIVE OIL

SOUPE AU PISTOU

SERVES 6–8

100g dried beans, such
   as flageolet, cannellini
   or haricots, soaked
   overnight in cold water
4 tbsp olive oil
1 garlic clove, finely chopped
1 onion, chopped
1 leek, halved lengthways
   and finely sliced
2 carrots, chopped
1 bouquet garni
   (bay leaf, thyme sprigs
   and parsley stalks)
675g courgettes,
   cut into small dice
450g tomatoes, skinned,
   seeded and chopped
2 medium potatoes,
   cut into small dice
100g fine green beans,
   topped, tailed and
   cut into 3–4 pieces
100g frozen peas
75g orzo or spaghetti,
   broken into small lengths
Salt and black pepper

To serve
Green pistou (page 302)
Grated Parmesan cheese
Extra virgin olive oil

Drain the soaked beans. Heat 2 tablespoons of the oil in a pan, add the garlic and cook gently for 2–3 minutes. Add the beans and 1.25 litres of water, bring to the boil, cover and simmer for 30–60 minutes, or until just tender. Add half a teaspoon of salt and simmer for another 5 minutes, then set aside.

Heat the remaining oil in a large pan. Add the onion, leek and carrots and cook gently for 5–6 minutes until softened but not browned. Add the beans, their cooking liquor and the bouquet garni to the pan of softened vegetables. Add the courgettes, tomatoes and potatoes and another 1.25 litres of water, then season with 2 teaspoons of salt and some pepper. Bring to the boil and simmer, uncovered, for 20 minutes.

Add the green beans, peas and pasta to the pan and simmer for another 10 minutes or until the pasta is cooked.

Remove the pan from the heat, take out the bouquet garni and stir in the pistou. Check the seasoning and serve in warmed bowls, with some extra grated Parmesan cheese and a little jug of extra virgin olive oil to drizzle on top.

This recipe comes from an extraordinarily comfortable hotel in the village of Trémolat in the Dordogne, where the French film director Claude Chabrol and his wife Stéphane Audran stayed while filming *Le Boucher*. This book isn't a food guide but the restaurant at this hotel is well worth a visit, except that you will be in the company of many an English couple who've arrived in their Jags and are probably worshipping the memory of Audran. For my own money, I would have sooner enjoyed this soup in a small, family-run bistro but the chef, Vincent Arnould, prepared it with singular skill.

VIEUX LOGIS GARLIC SOUP
SOUPE À L'AIL

SERVES 4

50g duck fat
100g garlic cloves,
    chopped
25g plain flour
1 litre Chicken stock
    (page 301)
3 eggs, separated
1 tsp sherry vinegar
4 slices stale white
    sourdough bread
4 tsp walnut oil
Salt and black pepper

Melt the duck fat in a large pan. Add the garlic and fry it gently for 5 minutes over a low heat until softened, but not browned. Add the flour and cook for a minute or so, then gradually add the stock, whisking after each addition to avoid lumps. Bring to the boil and skim the surface, then add a teaspoon of salt and cook for 10 minutes.

Lightly whisk the egg whites and trickle them into the soup, stirring so they form strands. Cook gently for 2–3 minutes. Mix the egg yolks with the vinegar in a bowl and season with plenty of black pepper. Add a ladleful of the hot soup to the bowl and stir, then add another ladleful of soup and keep stirring. Now add the yolk mixture to the pan of soup and immediately take the pan off the heat so the eggs don't curdle. Stir until thickened. Check the seasoning and add more if necessary.

Warm 4 bowls and put a slice of bread in each, then ladle over the soup. Add a swirl of walnut oil.

Pulse-based stews or soups in France are always special for me. One of the things I envy about French cooking is the enormous variety of dried beans available. Of these, Soissons blanc are held to be the biggest. They originate from the town of Soissons in Picardy and the story goes that they were first brought from Spain to the Abbey of Saint-Léger in the 18th century. As with Jersey Royals, putting a name to a bean or a potato gives it more character than just any old bean or spud.

WHITE BEAN & THYME SOUP

SOUPE AUX HARICOTS BLANCS ET THYM

SERVES 4

225g dried white beans
   (preferably Soissons
   from Picardy), soaked
   overnight in cold water
100g smoked bacon lardons
1 bay leaf
2 or 3 fresh thyme sprigs
2 tbsp vegetable or olive oil
30g butter
1 medium onion, chopped
1 large leek, chopped
2 celery sticks, chopped
1 large clove garlic, chopped
150ml whole milk
Handful flatleaf
   parsley, chopped
Salt and black pepper

Drain the soaked beans and put them in a large pan with 1.5 litres of fresh water, the lardons, bay leaf and thyme. Bring to the boil and skim off any foam that rises to the surface, then turn the heat down to a simmer and cook for about 30 minutes.

Heat the oil and butter in a separate pan and gently cook the onion, leek, celery and garlic until softened. Add them to the partially cooked beans and continue to cook for another 1–1¼ hours or so, until the beans are really tender.

Spoon about a third of the beans and some of the liquid into a blender and blitz until smooth. Tip this back into pan, add the milk, then stir well and warm through. Season with salt and plenty of pepper. Stir in the parsley just before serving with some crusty bread.

This recipe was given to me by Marty Freriksen, a Dutchman who owns the Château de Vaulx at Saint-Julien-de-Civry in Burgundy. He made the soup for me in his kitchen from sorrel that he'd grown in his vegetable garden. If you're travelling that way, the Château is a great place to stay. It's one of those massive rambling buildings where one room with a vast fireplace leads on to another, then another, then you find yourself in a part of the house you've never been in before. My bedroom, I remember, had three other bedrooms leading off it, and a bath that was fit for a titan!

MARTY'S SORREL SOUP FROM CHÂTEAU DE VAULX
SOUPE À L'OSEILLE

SERVES 4–6

50g butter
1 large onion, chopped
2 cloves garlic,
    roughly chopped
1 leek, halved lengthways,
    washed and sliced
450g potatoes, cut into
    rough 2cm cubes
1 litre Chicken or Vegetable
    stock (page 301)
250g sorrel, washed
1 tbsp honey
4 tbsp single cream
1 tbsp chopped chives
Salt and black pepper

Melt the butter in a large pan and add the onion, garlic, leek and potatoes. Cook over a medium heat for about 15 minutes until the vegetables have softened.

Add the stock and the sorrel and cook for 15–20 minutes over a medium heat until the potatoes are tender. Blend until smooth.

Season with salt and plenty of black pepper, then stir in the honey. Ladle the soup into warmed bowls and add a swirl of cream and some freshly chopped chives. Serve with warm crusty bread.

Freshly picked white crab meat has become increasingly expensive and hard to get hold of, mostly because Asia seems to have woken up to how exquisite our native brown crabs are – and they are exported live. The less you do to crab the better I always think, but this simple salad of white meat with the brown mixed in a let-down mayonnaise for a dressing is, dare I say it, pretty special. There's a recipe for my mustard mayonnaise on page 302. Incidentally, if you mix some very finely shredded celeriac with white crab meat it makes it go further and it's very hard to tell which is which. I'd suggest using a maximum of one-third celeriac to two-thirds of crab meat.

CRAB SALAD WITH FENNEL & ASPARAGUS

SERVES 4
as a starter or
2 as a light lunch

100g asparagus tips
4 tbsp Mustard mayonnaise
   (page 302)
50g brown crab meat
½ tsp lemon juice
80g butterhead lettuce
1 small fennel bulb
   (about 150g) trimmed
   and very finely sliced
120g white crab meat
8 chives, chopped
   on the diagonal
2–3 tarragon sprigs,
   leaves roughly chopped
1 lemon, cut into wedges
Salt and black pepper

Steam the asparagus tips until tender, then refresh them under cold water and set aside.

Mix the mayonnaise with the brown crab meat in a bowl, stirring well to get rid of any lumps. Add the lemon juice and about 2 teaspoons of water to make it runny enough to use as a dressing. Season with salt and pepper.

Divide the butterhead lettuce, sliced fennel and asparagus tips between your plates. Dress the salad with the brown crab mayonnaise, then top with the white crab meat. Finish with the chopped chives, tarragon and lemon wedges.

In Collioure, I quickly came to realise that this little salad sums up what's best about French Mediterranean cuisine. It's the sort of thing you can rustle up so easily, whether as an appetiser, a simple first course or light lunch and everyone will love it, unless they don't like anchovies that is; there are some poor, misguided people who don't get the satisfying saltiness of them. Interestingly, presentation of this salad around Collioure varies from rather silly stripe arrangements to towers, but I have never been a great fan of tower food and clock arrangements – not my kind of thing – and prefer to keep it simple. By the way, the anchovies in the Languedoc-Roussillon region are really quite special and it's worth spending money on them for this dish. Cheap anchovies are for stews or dips. *Recipe photograph overleaf.*

SALAD OF PEPPERS, ANCHOVIES & HARD-BOILED EGGS

SALADE COLLIOURE

SERVES 4

4 large red peppers
Small handful flatleaf
   parsley, finely chopped
1 clove garlic, finely chopped
1–2 tbsp olive oil
4 eggs, hard-boiled
   and peeled
12 salted anchovy fillets
   (from Collioure if possible)
1 padrón pepper, seeded
   and cut into matchsticks
   or good pinch of chilli
   flakes (optional)
Basil leaves
Salt and black pepper

Preheat the oven to 220°C/Fan 200°C. Put the red peppers on a baking tray and roast them for 25–30 minutes until charred, turning them over halfway through. Transfer them to a bowl, cover with a lid or a plate and leave them to steam until cool. Peel off the charred skin, then cut each pepper in half and scoop out the seeds. Trim off the stalks and discard those and the seeds. Slice the pepper flesh into ½cm-wide strips and place them in a clean bowl. Season with salt and pepper.

Mix the finely chopped parsley and garlic with the olive oil and season with salt and pepper.

When ready to serve, make a nest of red pepper strips on each plate and top with a hard-boiled egg. Place 3 salted anchovy fillets over each egg and dot the plate with a little of the parsley mixture. Lastly, add a few matchsticks of padrón pepper or chilli flakes, if using, and a few basil leaves.

I met Renée Michon, a leading light in L'Association des Pêcheurs à Pied, by the rather splendid green and white lighthouse at La Pointe du Hourdel at the beginning of the Baie de Somme. We had organised a morning of foraging for oreilles de cochon, sea asters, also known as asters de mer in France – a rather less colourful name than pigs' ears. We were also on the hunt for sea purslane and, though perhaps a little early, marsh samphire. As it turned out, most of the crew lost their boots in the mud, and Pete, the sound recordist, fell over in it too. Renée, a fit-looking 60-year-old with a robust sense of humour, was unperturbed, presumably having seen such things happen many times before. The oreilles proved the most abundant of our finds. 'Fishing on foot' is taking off in the UK too and I must say I really enjoyed the experience. I came away, boots still on, with this recipe, which Renée prepared in a restaurant on the waterfront. Sea asters are available for a short season in early summer from a few supermarkets and speciality suppliers, but the salad is also really good with samphire or sea purslane. If you use samphire, it may need blanching, unless it's very young.

NEW POTATO & SEA ASTER SALAD
SALADE DE POMMES DE TERRE ET ASTERS MARITIMES

SERVES 4
as a side salad

400g waxy new potatoes,
  such as Jersey Royals
2 handfuls sea asters
  (see suppliers, page 309)
  or samphire
1 small red onion,
  finely sliced
Salt

Dressing
4 tbsp rapeseed
  or sunflower oil
1 tbsp red wine vinegar
1 tsp Dijon mustard
½ tsp salt
¼ tsp caster sugar

Scrub the potatoes well or peel them, then boil them in salted water until tender. Drain and cut them in half if large. Mix the ingredients for the dressing.

If using samphire, blanch it in boiling water for 1–2 minutes, then drain. The sea asters can be used raw.

Toss the warm potatoes with the sliced onion and the sea asters or samphire, then mix with the dressing. Serve warm or at room temperature.

In line with a general feeling that salades composées are an important part of a French restaurant menu, I came up with this recipe. It's a melange of the kind of things I like to find in a salad. *Recipe photograph overleaf.*

LENTIL, BEETROOT & GOATS' CHEESE SALAD
SALADE DE LENTILLES, BETTERAVE ET CHÈVRE

SERVES 2
as a main course
or 4 as a starter

175g small beetroots,
    washed but not peeled
2 tbsp olive oil
1 shallot, finely chopped
1 garlic clove, finely chopped
100g Puy lentils, rinsed
1 fresh thyme sprig
Small handful flatleaf
    parsley, chopped
1 ripe pear
100g goats' cheese log
2 small handfuls
    rocket leaves
4 walnut halves,
    roughly chopped
Salt and black pepper

Dressing
2 tbsp olive oil
1 tbsp walnut oil
1 tbsp Banyuls
    or sherry vinegar

Preheat the oven to 190°C/Fan 170°C. Put the beetroots on a baking tray and roast them for up to an hour, depending on size. They should be tender to the point of a knife when done. Leave them until cool enough to handle, then peel off the skins and cut them into wedges. Set aside.

Heat the olive oil in a pan and sweat the shallot and garlic over a medium heat until softened. Add the lentils, 300ml of water, thyme, half a teaspoon of salt and plenty of black pepper, then simmer for 23 minutes. You may need to add a little more water, but the object is for it all to become absorbed. Leave the lentils to cool down, then add the chopped parsley.

Core and slice the pear, leaving the skin on. Cut the cheese in half horizontally or into 4 slices, depending on how many you are serving. Preheat the grill and grill the cheese on one side. Mix the olive oil, walnut oil and vinegar to make the dressing.

Put the lentils in a wide dish, then top with some rocket leaves. Nestle beetroot wedges and pear slices among the leaves and top with the grilled goats' cheese and dressing. Sprinkle over the walnuts and serve at once.

Virtually any place you stop for lunch in France these days will have some sort of what I call a main course salad on the menu. My wife and virtually every female I know goes for these, but so do I, and when you're touring and eating a fair bit they're a godsend. There's always salade niçoise, a Caesar, of course, with chargrilled chicken, and in the southwest, to ring the changes, there might be ham and cheese plus duck gizzards, called gésiers. Sadly, though, the ingredients are too often predictable: a packet of mixed leaves, slices of ham, cheese, tomatoes, sometimes a boiled egg and a balsamic vinegar dressing. All you can say about such a salad is that there's plenty of it, but it's not that difficult to be a bit inventive. This salad is the sort of thing I would like to see on a menu somewhere. No unusual ingredients but there are fried chicken livers, which I love, and a warm dressing made by deglazing the pan in which you have cooked the livers. A salade tiède in other words.

WARM CHICKEN LIVER, BACON & ORANGE SALAD

SALADE TIÈDE DE FOIE DE VOLAILLES À L'ORANGE

SERVES 4

400g waxy new potatoes
2 small oranges
100g smoked bacon lardons
    or cubed pancetta
1½ tbsp butter
200g fresh chicken livers,
    trimmed of sinew and
    cut into bite-sized pieces
100g baby spinach,
    washed and spun dry
100g radicchio or
    chicory, trimmed
10 chives, snipped into
    2cm lengths
1-2 tbsp hazelnuts, toasted
    and roughly chopped
Black pepper

Dressing

1 tbsp Banyuls or
    sherry vinegar
1 tbsp orange juice
3 tbsp chicken stock
3 tbsp olive oil
Salt and black pepper

Scrub the potatoes well or peel them, then boil in salted water until tender. Cut them in half if large and keep them warm.

While the potatoes are cooking, segment the oranges. Cut off the top and bottom of the orange. Stand the orange on a board and, using a sharp knife, cut away the skin and all the white pith. Holding the fruit over a bowl to catch any juice, cut along the sides of each segment to release them from the membrane. Squeeze any juice from the membranes and use it for the dressing. Mix all the ingredients for the dressing together.

In a frying pan, fry the lardons or pancetta until crisp, then remove them and set aside. Add the butter to the bacon fat in the pan and fry the livers for 2 minutes on each side, then set them aside. Add the dressing to the pan to deglaze it and warm the dressing.

Arrange the spinach and radicchio or chicory on a large dish. Top with the warm potatoes, lardons or pancetta, orange segments and chicken livers. Scatter over the chives and hazelnuts, season with a little black pepper and drizzle over the warm dressing. Serve immediately.

While watching Céline Josmeyer make this confit duck and lentil salad, I was thinking how complete is the relationship between wine and food in France. This dish, so spare in its ingredients and speedy in its production, is designed to go with Josmeyers Pinot Gris 1854 from the famous Alsace vignerons. I tried both at the same time and can confirm that the match is perfect.

WARM SALAD OF LENTILS & DUCK CONFIT
SALADE TIÈDE DE LENTILLES ET CONFIT DE CANARD

SERVES 4

2 Confit duck legs
(page 303 or bought)
2 tbsp olive oil
2 carrots, finely diced
4 celery sticks, trimmed
and finely diced
240g Puy lentils, rinsed
and drained
1 medium onion, peeled
and studded with 6 cloves
2 bay leaves
Salt and black pepper

Herb vinaigrette
4 tbsp olive oil
1½ tbsp Melfor vinegar or
1½ tbsp red wine vinegar
plus 1 tsp runny honey
1 small shallot, very
finely chopped
Handful flatleaf parsley,
finely chopped

Put the confit legs in a pan, cover and heat gently to melt the fat and warm the meat through. Pour off the fat and keep it for roast potatoes. Transfer the duck to a board and pull the meat apart with your fingers or a couple of forks. Discard the bones.

Heat the oil in a pan and sweat the carrots and celery over a medium heat until softened. Add the lentils, 500ml of water, the clove-studded onion and the bay leaves, then season with a teaspoon of salt and plenty of black pepper. Simmer for 23 minutes. You may need to add a little more water, but the object is for it all to become absorbed. Discard the onion and bay leaves.

Whisk together the vinaigrette ingredients and season with salt and plenty of black pepper.

Mix the lentils and shredded duck meat in a large bowl and dress with the vinaigrette. Serve warm or at room temperature.

I can't remember where this recipe came from. It's a bit of me and a bit of life on the road, but I do remember thinking at the time that it's in these sort of salads that all the wonderful fresh produce you see in the market ends up. What do the French do with their lovely vegetables? Now I know: they make nice salads at home. *Recipe photograph overleaf.*

SALAD OF NEW POTATOES, GREEN BEANS, EGGS & ARTICHOKES

SALADE DE POMMES DE TERRE, HARICOTS VERTS, OEUFS ET ARTICHAUTS

SERVES 4
as a main course

400g waxy new potatoes
220g fine green beans
125g frisée lettuce
4 cooked artichoke hearts
    (or use a jar of artichoke
    hearts), halved
4 hard-boiled eggs,
    peeled and halved
2 slices of sourdough bread,
    cubed and made into
    croutons (page 303)
12 chives, chopped
4 tbsp Classic vinaigrette
    (page 302)
Salt and black pepper

Scrub the potatoes well or peel them, then boil in salted water until tender. Cut them in half if large and leave to cool. Boil the green beans in salted water for 4-5 minutes, then drain them and refresh with cold water.

Arrange the frisée lettuce on a large shallow dish. Add the new potatoes, green beans, artichokes, eggs and croutons. Season with salt and pepper and scatter over the chives. Dress with vinaigrette just before serving.

I got this pungent fennel sauce from Paul Griffon, whose cookery classes teach uncompromising Provençal cooking like the beef stew on page 210. Flavoured with fennel seeds and garlic, this is almost too intense on its own but, like anchoïade or tapenade, it makes an excellent dip for such things as carrot sticks, radishes, artichoke leaves or warm new potatoes.

FENNEL DIP
FENOUILLADE

MAKES A SMALL BOWLFUL

100g whole blanched
   almonds
10g capers, drained
   and rinsed
2 salted anchovies
1 tsp fennel seeds,
   roughly ground
1 clove garlic, chopped
1 tsp red wine vinegar
90ml olive oil
1 tbsp warm water

Put the almonds, capers, anchovies, fennel seeds, garlic and vinegar in a food processor and pulse as for a pesto. Don't over process, as the mixture should have some texture.

Add the olive oil and water, then spoon into a bowl and serve with raw vegetables.

The village of Trizac is in the Cantal department of the Auvergne in south-central France. It is exactly the sort of village I referred to in the main introduction, somewhere in the beautiful vastness of rural France. The population has decreased from 1,200 in the early 1960s to 500 now, and as with so many similar places you can't believe how exquisite a small collection of buildings with a Romanesque church can be. It is almost inevitable to me that an area of France so remote should have a terrine like this one. I watched it being made in the butchers' shop run by Patrick and Sophie Bornes in the village with a growing feeling that this really wouldn't translate – it was, after all, a mixture of pork, prunes and chard in a curious batter with lots of eggs – but how wrong can you be! It's what one might call a peasant dish that mixes sweet and salty and looks really interesting, larded with coarse pork meat and prunes and coloured with the green leaves of chard. The locals recommend it with a cold beer or a glass of wine and I have been doing just that while writing this. It's also excellent as a light lunch with some salad.

HAM & CHARD TERRINE

POUNTI

SERVES 10–12
(as a nibble with drinks)

60g lard, melted, plus
   extra for greasing
100g smoked bacon lardons
1 onion, chopped
150g self-raising flour
1 tsp salt
3 eggs
130ml whole milk
125g Swiss chard, well
   washed, tough stalks
   removed and chopped
100g cured ham, such as
   Bayonne or Parma
100g pulled ham hock meat,
   or baked ham chopped
16 semi-dried prunes
Handful flatleaf parsley,
   chopped
Black pepper

Thoroughly grease a non-stick loaf tin or terrine mould, measuring about 24 x 10 x 6cm, with lard and line the base with a strip of baking parchment.

Heat a little of the lard in a small frying pan over a medium heat. Add the bacon lardons, then the onion and fry gently until softened but not browned. Leave to cool while you make the batter. Preheat the oven to 180°C/Fan 160°C.

Mix the flour and salt in a large bowl. Whisk in the eggs and when smooth, gradually add the milk and then the melted lard. Season with black pepper, then add the cooked onion and lardons, the chopped chard, cured ham, ham hock, prunes and parsley and mix well.

Turn the mixture into the tin or mould and bake for about 45 minutes. Leave it to cool in the tin before turning out and cutting into slices.

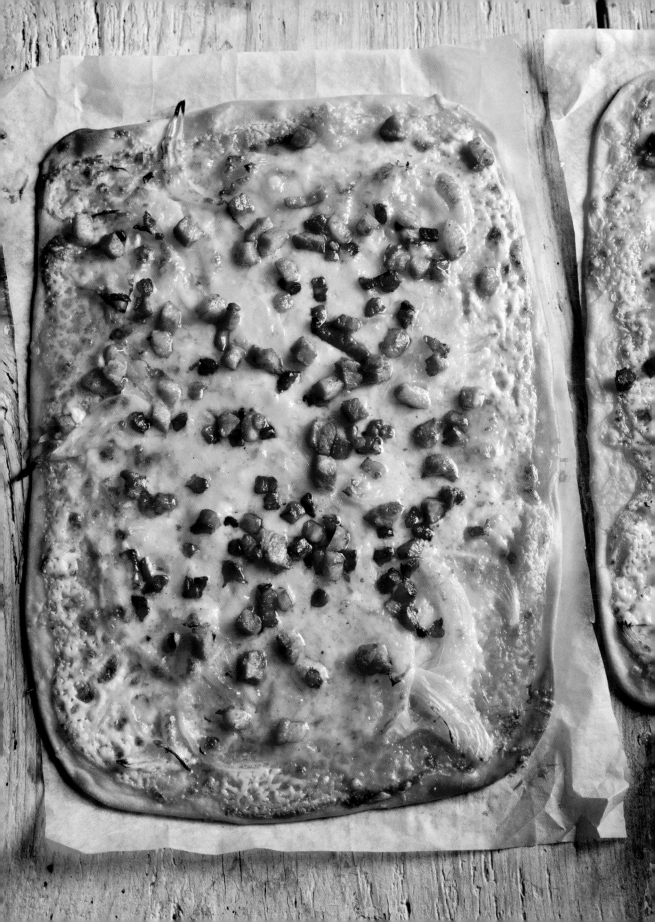

I was first introduced to tarte flambée with the explanation that it's France's answer to pizza. In fact, though, it's not much like pizza at all, apart from being very thin and savoury, and as it is made with unleavened dough it bakes very crisply indeed, which is its great quality. Like pizza, it's best baked in a wood oven, especially when the wood embers are pushed aside from the base of the oven and slightly burn the edges – hence the name tarte flambée, or in Alsace, where the dish comes from, flammekueche. I know you can get tarte flambée in London but why it isn't as famous as pizza escapes me. It's just as good, almost better dare I say, when made with bacon lardons and Emmental or Gruyère. It comes in big discs or rectangles, but I find the rectangles are more convenient, as you can fit two on a standard domestic oven baking sheet.

FRENCH 'PIZZA' OF CHEESE & HAM

TARTE FLAMBÉE

SERVES 4–12
depending on whether
a light lunch or snacks
with drinks

Dough
250g plain flour, sifted,
   plus extra for dusting
½ tsp salt
150ml tepid water
2 tbsp sunflower oil

Topping
250g full-fat crème fraiche
1 large onion, finely sliced
160g smoked bacon lardons,
   fried until browned
250g Emmental or
   Gruyère cheese
   or a mixture, grated
A few rasps freshly
   grated nutmeg
Salt and black pepper

Mix the flour and salt in a bowl, then add the water and oil and bring everything together to make rough dough. Transfer the dough to a floured board and knead well. Roll the dough into 2 rectangles, each measuring about 25 x 28cm.

Preheat the oven to 230°C/Fan 210°C or as hot as your oven will go. Spread the crème fraiche over the dough, leaving a little border around the edges, then dot with the onion, lardons and grated cheese. Season with salt, pepper and nutmeg.

Bake for 10–12 minutes or until the base is crisp and the cheese is bubbling. Slide the tarts on to a wooden board and use a pizza cutter to cut them into portions. Serve immediately with drinks or as a light lunch with a green salad.

My wife Sas loves snails in garlic butter almost more than anything else, apart from perhaps oysters. And I must say that when I was offered them as a sort of incidental snack while sampling some delicious white Burgundy in the cellars of Eric Bonnetain in Auxey-Duresses, it was a moment of revelation. Tasting a dish that was the stock-in-trade of any French bistro in the UK in the 1960s, 70s and 80s but made with the snails that live on the local vines and were cooked with fresh parsley, butter and local garlic was to revisit the first time I ever ate them. I read of an experiment recently where two batches of oysters were served: one with the music of the countryside, birdsong, breezes and so on, and the other with the sounds of the sea and seagulls. The preference for the latter was overwhelming, even though it was revealed that they were the same oysters. Those snails and the balance of chardonnay and oak in the Meursault complimented each other astoundingly, and surely this was down to the localness of the snails. My recipe is for tinned ones and most important is to use lots of garlic, plenty of fresh parsley and, in my opinion, salted butter. Snails and shells are readily available online.

SNAILS IN GARLIC BUTTER
ESCARGOTS AU BEURRE D'AIL

SERVES 4
as a starter or appetiser

24 large snails and
    24 empty shells
1 shallot, roughly chopped
Leaves from 40g
    flatleaf parsley
85g salted butter, softened
4-5 garlic cloves, crushed
    or very finely chopped
1 small baguette, sliced
Salt and black pepper

Drain and rinse the snails, then leave them to dry in a colander. Preheat the oven to 200°C/Fan 180°C.

Chop the shallot and parsley leaves together finely (use the stems in stock). Mix the softened butter with the shallot and parsley and the garlic. Season with salt and plenty of pepper, then continue to mix really well until you have a green, very garlicky butter. Put a little in the bottom of each shell, then add a snail and fill with more of the butter.

Nestle the filled shells on a bed of baking beans or crumpled greaseproof paper in an ovenproof dish or roasting tin. It's important to keep the shells steady so they don't tip over and spill their garlic butter. If you prefer, use ramekins, putting 6 snails in each one, again on a bed of beans or crumpled greaseproof paper.

Bake the snails for 15 minutes, then serve immediately with some baguette to mop up the garlicky juices.

In the 1980s, I used to have a version of this dish on the menu every day at The Seafood Restaurant in Padstow. It was the perfect vehicle for the mussels from the Camel Estuary, which I used to get picked in hessian sackfuls and then purify them myself in the old coach house behind our house on Trevose Head on my day off. The Padstow mussels are unusual in that they are what the French call moules d'Espagne, though how they got from Spain to Padstow nobody knows – probably on the keel of a ship. They're a bit of a delicacy in the Catalan region of France and I had a similar dish to this at a fish restaurant in Port-Vendres, just near the border with Spain. In the old days, I used to try to write my menu in French and this dish was called moules au beurre d'escargot. It's not been on since, but I think I've improved it by adding breadcrumbs and Emmental.

GRILLED MUSSELS WITH SNAIL BUTTER

SERVES 4
as a starter

100ml dry cider
or dry white wine
48 large mussels,
cleaned and debearded
Large handful
flatleaf parsley
2–3 cloves garlic
2 tbsp olive oil, plus
extra for drizzling
30g butter, softened
20g panko breadcrumbs
25g Emmental cheese,
finely grated
Lemon wedges
Salt and black pepper

Bring the cider or wine to the boil in a large pan. Add the mussels, put a lid on the pan and steam the mussels open for 3–4 minutes. Drain them in a sieve over a bowl and reserve the juice. Tip the juice back into the pan and reduce it over a high heat to 2 tablespoons.

Separate the shells, discarding the empty halves, and arrange the mussels in their half shells on a baking tray.

Chop the parsley with the garlic fairly finely and put them in a bowl. Add the cider or wine reduction, olive oil and butter, then mix to make a paste. Season with salt and pepper.

Preheat the grill to its hottest setting. Spoon the paste over the mussels, then mix the breadcrumbs with the grated Emmental and sprinkle on top. Drizzle with more oil. Place the mussels under the hot grill and cook until the breadcrumbs are golden brown. Serve immediately with lemon wedges.

The Étang de Leucate is a saltwater lagoon just north of Perpignan and famous for its oysters. I asked Jérôme Ferrari to prepare a platter of oysters, raw mussels and palourdes, all grown in the Étang, at his processing shed for my lunch. There were about 20 similar shacks bordering the water at Grau de Leucate and all had seafood bars attached to them. By lunchtime all were full and none of them sold anything but platters of fruits de mer and very few other wines than Picpoul de Pinet, the lovely fruity but fresh-tasting white wine of the Languedoc.

Jérôme grows huîtres de la Caramoun, using a method that gives them a matchless flavour. He attaches each oyster to ropes that are suspended in the water, but to make them work harder, like the best vines in stony subsoil, he regularly raises the ropes out of the water for several hours so the oysters become hardier and thereby better flavoured. Indeed, at the Salon d'Agriculture in Paris he won a silver medal in competition with oysters from all over France the first time he entered. Some talk about the oysters as having an incomparable taste, which persists for a long time in the mouth, and a faint aroma of hazelnut; the inner shell has a slight tinge of pink. Sampling the oysters back at his seafood shack, the unique freshness, saltiness and taste of the sea was quite clear, though I couldn't quite pick up the hazelnuts.

To me, all this epitomises the way the French go that little bit further to achieve unforgettable flavour. Roquefort, Château d'Yquem, Charolais beef – everywhere there is evidence of the work of generations of artisans. I guess I've been guilty in the past of making unpopular comparisons between French seafood and our own, and indeed a feast of cockles and jellied eels in Leigh-on-Sea in Essex or a pile of langoustines on the west coast of Scotland are just as spontaneously enjoyable as those oysters, but the French passion for seafood goes pretty deep.

Because of the meandering nature of my journey through France this time, described by David Pritchard as 'the mark of Zorro', I didn't pass along as much of the French coastline as I would have liked. I did, though, have plenty of great seafood in the restaurants all along the harbour in Dieppe, through Normandy and on to Picardy and Le Crotoy in the Bay of the Somme. Much later in Collioure and Port-Vendres on the coast of Languedoc, there were sardines and anchovies in particular, and finally in Provence a memorable bouillabaisse in Cassis. This town is almost like a Greek island village with its jumble of pretty pink, yellow and blue houses fighting for space in the steep valley that ends in the port.

This is almost not a recipe, but when we were filming at a remarkably unusual restaurant called Le Cabaret, the chef and owner Antoine Delmas produced this as part of a multi-course menu – slightly on the hoof. In other words, the courses came out of the kitchen, which was part of the dining room, haphazardly and the flow slowed down if Antoine felt like coming over and having a chat and a glass of wine. If you go on any TripAdvisor-type website, you'll see that the words outlandish, quirky and boozy are often mentioned, and even the normally tight-lipped Michelin guide expresses unusual personal enthusiasm for the restaurant, which is in Montesquieu-des-Albères, Languedoc-Roussillon. There's no menu and you might never get in because the restaurant is always booked, but it's the sort of place you'll never forget. I particularly liked this dish. You couldn't really serve it as anything but a tiny course in between many others, but it really concentrates the mind on the sweet flavour of mussels with the suggestion of olive oil and pepper in the background. This is one of those occasions when a special black pepper is called for, such as Kampot pepper from Cambodia or Wayanad from Kerala. Both are available online.

VERY SIMPLE MUSSELS

MOULES FACILES

SERVES 4

48 large fresh mussels,
   scrubbed and debearded
2 tbsp Provençal olive oil
Black pepper

Heat 50ml of water in a large pan and bring it to the boil, then throw in the mussels. Put a lid on the pan and steam the mussels for 3–4 minutes until opened. Drain them over a bowl to collect the juice.

Put the mussels in a large serving bowl, dress them with the oil, black pepper and a couple of tablespoons of the cooking liquor, then toss well to distribute the seasoning. Serve immediately.

Saint-Valery-sur-Somme is a pretty little town on the Baie de Somme, which is where William the Conqueror set out from with his fleet to invade England. It's also famous for its rope-grown mussels (moules de bouchot), as are many places along the coast of Normandy and the Somme. With these thoughts, I enthusiastically ordered this dish at a hotel with a view right across the bay to the town of Le Crotoy. What could be a better lunch, I thought, except that the mussels were not at all great; a bit smelly, in fact. So, to restore the pleasant thoughts of sweet mussels and the cream, butter and cider of the area, here's a recipe complete with chicken stock and a few bacon lardons for good measure. *Recipe photograph overleaf.*

MUSSELS WITH POULETTE SAUCE

MOULES SAUCE POULETTE

SERVES 6
as a starter, 3–4 as a main

40g butter
75g unsmoked bacon lardons
2 shallots, finely chopped
1 bay leaf
1 fresh thyme sprig
200ml dry cider
225ml Chicken stock
   (page 301)
2kg mussels, scrubbed
   and debearded
225g full-fat crème fraiche
1 egg yolk
Juice of ¼ lemon
Small handful flatleaf
   parsley, chopped
Salt and black pepper

Melt the butter in a pan. Add the bacon lardons and shallots and fry them over a medium heat until the shallots are soft but not coloured. Add the bay leaf, thyme and cider, then cook until the liquid is reduced by half.

Add the stock and bring to the boil, then add the mussels. Cover the pan with a lid and steam the mussels for 4–5 minutes until they've all opened. Using a slotted spoon, remove the mussels and set them aside to keep them warm while you finish the sauce.

Mix the crème fraiche with the egg yolk and a ladleful of the stock in a bowl. With the pan over a low to medium heat, whisk the mixture into the cooking liquid, keeping an eye on it to prevent the sauce from splitting. Don't allow it to come to the boil. Season with salt and pepper and add the lemon juice and half the parsley.

Put the mussels back in the pan and stir to coat them in the sauce. Spoon into warmed bowls and garnish with the remaining parsley. Serve with hunks of warm bread to mop up the juices.

This recipe comes from Les Templiers, a bar in Collioure, southern France. I particularly liked it because I thought I'd personally evolved the way of baking fish in the oven on a bed of vegetables, including such things as sliced potatoes, tomatoes and garlic. I'd worked out that you had to precook the vegetables, otherwise the fish would be absurdly overcooked, and at Les Templiers they do exactly that. The dish comes with the fish already taken off the bone – everything you would expect from a good restaurant in a seaside town in the Languedoc – but you can serve it whole if you prefer. It's actually the bar where Patrick O'Brian, the novelist who wrote so many wonderful books about the British navy in Napoleonic times, used to go. It's adorned with great paintings, not only downstairs but also in the private dining room upstairs, and there's the odd one by Picasso, who was also a regular. I enjoyed the thought of Patrick, who was something of a recluse, and Pablo, who was anything but, at Les Templiers – Picasso at one end of the bar full of life and drinking and smoking with his chums, and Patrick at the other end, head down and lost in thought.

BAKED WHOLE BREAM WITH POTATOES

POISSON FAÇON À LA PAULINE

SERVES 4

400g waxy potatoes, scrubbed and sliced into 5mm rounds
60ml olive oil
3 large tomatoes, sliced into 5mm thick rounds
20 black olives, pitted
4 large garlic cloves, skin on and bruised
2-4 whole bream (depending on size), scaled, cleaned and gutted but left whole
1 lemon
½ tsp Rick's peppermix (page 303)
Salt and black pepper

Preheat the oven to 190°C/Fan 170°C. Toss the sliced potatoes with half of the oil in a roasting tin large enough to fit them in a single layer. Season the potatoes with salt and pepper and bake for 15 minutes.

Add the sliced tomatoes, olives and garlic, then lay the fish on top. Drizzle with the remaining olive oil and a squeeze of lemon juice, then season with the peppermix. Put the tin back in the oven and bake for about 25 minutes.

Transfer the bream to a large plate and drizzle with a little more oil and lemon juice if desired. Squeeze the garlic flesh out of the skins over the vegetables. Serve the fish whole or off the bone with the vegetables and a green salad on the side.

À la plancha is the Spanish way of quickly cooking molluscs, prawns and small pieces of fish and it's really caught on in Catalan France. The Spanish term is a rather romantic way of describing what we would call a griddle – a large, thick piece of steel heated from below. It's difficult to achieve this cooking method at home because of the need to have a big slab of metal in your kitchen; otherwise you need a large thick-bottomed pan or a casserole dish to ensure plenty of residual heat. The idea for this recipe came from a morning out with oyster man Jérôme Ferrari, who has a concession to farm oysters in the Étang de Leucate, a saltwater lake in the Pyrénées-Orientales. So far you cannot get these oysters in the UK, but I came up with this little recipe to celebrate palourdes, my favourite clams. This works equally well with mussels. You will need a heavy cast-iron frying pan.

CLAMS À LA PLANCHA WITH CONFIT GARLIC & SPINACH

SERVES 2
as a starter

100g spinach
25ml olive oil
20 palourde clams
 (300–350g), scrubbed
15g Confit garlic, roughly
 chopped (page 302)
Black pepper or a large
 pinch of Rick's peppermix
 (page 303)
Large pinch of piment
 d'Espelette (page 306)
 or pimentón

Wash the spinach and put it in a pan with the water that clings to the leaves. Allow it to wilt over a gentle heat, then drain well.

Heat a wide, heavy-based pan over a high heat until smoking hot. Throw in the oil and the clams and turn them over with a wooden spoon. As the clams open, allow the liquor from them to boil down to almost nothing. Just before the pan goes dry, remove it from the heat.

Add the spinach, confit garlic and seasoning and stir to coat the clams. Serve immediately with crusty bread.

This comes from a wonderfully hopeful, youthful idea. A couple of chefs who used to work in a three-Michelin-star restaurant have formed a little company based in Clermont-Ferrand. They travel the villages of the Auvergne in a double-decker bus; downstairs is the kitchen and upstairs the restaurant. The menu is three-Michelin-star standard and the execution little short of miraculous. Most of the prep is done back at base in the city but this is still an unbelievable achievement. This was my favourite dish. They made it with raw langoustine but I use lobster which is easier to find. If you would like to cook your own lobster, see page 306.

POACHED LOBSTER RISOTTO

RISOTTO AU HOMARD

SERVES 4
as a starter or 2 as a main

1 cooked lobster,
    about 500g
30ml olive oil
1 shallot, finely chopped
2 cloves garlic,
    finely chopped
200g Carnaroli or
    Arborio risotto rice
150ml dry white wine
1 tbsp butter
Fresh tarragon fronds,
    to garnish
Salt and black pepper

Lobster stock and reduction
Lobster shell, chopped
1 onion, chopped
4 cloves garlic, roughly
    chopped, no need
    to peel
50g butter
100ml dry white wine
500g tomatoes,
    roughly chopped
Small handful French
    tarragon, roughly chopped
1.5 litres Fish stock (page 301)
1 tsp salt
1 tbsp Cognac
Squeeze of lemon juice

Carefully remove the meat from the lobster, reserving the shell for the stock. Slice the body meat and keep the claw meat as chunky as possible.

For the stock, put the shell in a pan with the onion, garlic and 20g of the butter. Cook for about 5 minutes over a medium heat, stirring occasionally, then add the wine, tomatoes, tarragon and stock and bring to the boil. Add the salt and leave to simmer for 40 minutes. Pass the stock through a fine sieve over another large pan and discard the solid ingredients. Keep most of the stock for the risotto, but set aside 200ml for the reduction.

For the risotto, heat the oil in a pan, add the shallot and garlic and cook until soft. Add the rice and stir to coat it with the shallots and oil, then add the wine. Let it bubble and be absorbed by the rice, then start adding the hot stock, a ladleful at a time. Keep stirring and allow each ladleful to be absorbed before adding the next. When all the liquid has been added, taste and season as needed.

Meanwhile, finish the lobster reduction. Put the 200ml of stock you set aside into a clean pan with the Cognac and bring to the boil. Continue to cook until it's reduced by three-quarters, then whisk in the remaining 30g of butter to form a sauce that coats the back of a spoon. Add a squeeze of lemon juice.

Heat the tablespoon of butter in a frying pan. When it's foaming, add the lobster meat and warm it through. Serve the risotto topped with lobster meat and spoon the reduction around it. Garnish with fresh tarragon.

There's a large, very good fish shop on the quayside at Port-Vendres, which is between Collioure and Banyuls in the Languedoc-Roussillon. It used to be a thriving fishing port, but sadly because of overfishing there's now only one full-time trawler working there. It's run by Gabriel Diaz who goes out fishing every day and returns at 4pm to where his Spanish wife Maria José runs a little stall right by the water. She literally sells the fish to the public as Gabriel brings it in off the boat. The poissonnerie across the harbour still manages to stock a magnificent selection of fish and shellfish by buying from boats fishing in the Atlantic. The owner said to me that people come to places like Port-Vendres and expect red mullet, bass, dentex, John Dory, octopus and even things like those spiky sea snails called murex, so there's still plenty of business, even if it's not local. Upstairs they have a simple seafood bar where they sell things like grilled sardines, squid, fruits de mer and a few Catalan specialties, including prawn croquetas. I was particularly fond of these and what I liked was that they were really stuffed with good-quality prawns. I would suggest using the small North Atlantic peeled prawns, which are caught around Greenland.

PRAWN CROQUETAS

MAKES ABOUT 24 CROQUETAS
serves about 8 as tapas

85g butter
115g plain flour, plus
    extra for shaping
350ml whole milk
150ml double cream
250g small, North Atlantic
    cooked peeled prawns,
    chopped (defrosted
    and drained if frozen)
Salt and black pepper

For coating and cooking
700ml vegetable
    or sunflower oil
75g plain flour
2 eggs, beaten
175g panko breadcrumbs

Melt the butter in a pan over a medium heat. Add the flour and cook for a minute or so. Gradually add the milk and cream, whisking well all the time to ensure there are no lumps. Increase the heat slightly and bring the sauce to the boil. Turn the heat down and cook the sauce gently for 5 minutes, stirring often, by which time it should have thickened.

Stir in the chopped prawns, then season with a teaspoon of salt and plenty of black pepper. Spread this mixture out in a baking tray, cover the surface with a sheet of cling film or baking parchment and leave to cool. Then put the mixture in the fridge for 2 hours to firm up.

Heat the oil in a wide pan to 185°C. Put the 75g of flour, beaten eggs and breadcrumbs in 3 separate wide bowls. Using 2 dessertspoons, scoop out 8 lozenges of the mixture, each weighing about 20g, and drop them into the flour. Mould them with your hands into rough cork shapes and pass them into the beaten egg, then finally the breadcrumbs. Repeat with the rest of the mixture.

Lower 8 croquetas at a time into the hot oil and fry them for 2 minutes until they're crisp and lightly golden. Drain on kitchen paper and keep them warm while you cook the rest. Serve hot with drinks.

At the Bar Biquet on Plage Mouret this was the dish I particularly liked. It sounds kind of weird – octopus with beef gravy and a pile of olive oil mash – but it's only mar i muntanya, as the Catalans call it, or surf and turf for the Aussies. It was actually quite delicious and went down very well with the magnums of Provence rosé called Gris Blanc, which Biquet kept bringing over in 70s-style buckets made of highly oxidised dingy aluminium. These days the octopus you can buy is usually the common octopus (*Octopus vulgaris*), which is pretty tender. You can recognise it by the fact that it has twin rows of suckers on its tentacles. Don't be tempted to buy the curled or lesser octopus, identified by a single row of suckers, as it is far too tough and takes hours to cook to tender.

OCTOPUS WITH MASH & GRAVY

POULPE AU PURÉE DE POMMES DE TERRE ET SAUCE

SERVES 4
as a starter

250–300g small
   octopus tentacles
400g potatoes,
   cut into 5cm chunks
5 tbsp olive oil
1 onion, chopped
1 clove garlic, chopped
175ml red wine
400ml Rich beef stock
   (page 301)
Salt and black pepper

Bring a large pan of water to the boil. Add the octopus and a teaspoon of salt, then turn the heat down to a gentle simmer. Cook for about 45 minutes or until the tentacles are tender, then drain them and allow to cool. There's no need to skin them.

While the octopus is cooking, boil the potatoes in salted water until tender. Drain them very well and tip them back into the pan. Add 3 tablespoons of the oil and season with salt and pepper, then crush the potatoes with a fork, keeping some texture; they should not be completely smooth.

Heat the remaining 2 tablespoons of oil in a frying pan, add the onion and garlic and cook over a medium heat until softened. Add the red wine and beef stock and continue to cook until the liquid is reduced down to about 160ml (10–12 tablespoons). Pass this through a sieve and discard the onion and garlic. Return the liquid to the rinsed pan, add the octopus tentacles and heat for a couple of minutes, turning the tentacles over to glaze them with the sauce. Serve on top of the crushed potatoes.

I came up with this idea after a visit to Le Moulin de la Veyssière, in Périgord. It's a walnut and hazelnut oil mill, driven by water, and it's not only that it's in an absolutely beautiful part of France but there's also an almost film set atmosphere in the mill itself – wheels are whirring, belts are slapping and there's the background gurgling of water passing over the mill wheel. Both oils they produce are works of art. I've written this recipe for the walnut oil but I've included hazelnuts too, as I've often thought that scallops and hazelnuts have a great affinity. Hazelnut oil is much more expensive and harder to get hold of than walnut oil but if you are using it instead, use only two thirds of the amount.

SALAD OF SCALLOPS WITH GREEN BEANS
SALADE DE COQUILLES SAINT-JACQUES ET HARICOTS VERTS

SERVES 4
as a starter

150g haricots verts
   (thin French green
   beans), trimmed
2 small heads of chicory,
   yellow or red, trimmed
1 shallot, very finely chopped
¼ tsp caster sugar
½ tbsp sherry or
   balsamic vinegar
2 tbsp walnut oil
10 fresh cleaned scallops,
   with or without coral
1 tbsp olive or rapeseed oil
Good handful of pea shoots
20g whole hazelnuts,
   toasted lightly and
   roughly chopped
Salt and black pepper

Bring a pan of salted water to the boil, add the green beans and cook them for 4 minutes until they are tender but still with a bite. Drain the beans and refresh them in cold water to stop the cooking. Pull them apart lengthways, then put them in a bowl. Cut the chicory in half lengthways and then slice them thinly on the diagonal. Add them to the bowl with the green beans.

Mix the shallot with the sugar, vinegar and 2 tablespoons of the walnut oil and season with salt and pepper. Pour this mixture over the cooked beans and chicory and set aside.

Slice the scallops in half horizontally to make discs and pat them dry, then season with salt and pepper. Reserve any corals.

In a large non-stick frying pan, heat the olive or rapeseed oil over a moderately high heat until hot but not smoking. Sauté the scallops until golden – up to a minute on each side. Unless you have an enormous pan, cook the scallops in a couple of batches so you don't overcrowd the pan. Quickly cook the corals in the same way if you have them.

Divide the dressed beans and chicory between the plates and scatter over the pea shoots. Top each plate with 5 scallop discs and a couple of corals if you have them. Sprinkle over the chopped hazelnuts and drizzle over the remaining walnut oil. Season with more black pepper, then serve immediately.

This dish comes from a restaurant in Dieppe called Le Newhaven. I wonder if there are any restaurants called Le Dieppe in Newhaven! This was a good, but not must-visit, restaurant on the harbour, which also had some very lovely cheese, including Neufchâtel, Camembert and Pont L'Evêque. Actually the smell of cheese in many decent restaurants in France is what differentiates them from similar good restaurants in the UK, in this case not only ripe Camembert but also the bubbling Emmental on the fish gratin. I thought the accompanying sautéed apple might be a bit too 'Normande' for foreign consumption but it was actually really nice.

SEAFOOD GRATIN WITH CARAMELISED APPLES

SERVES 6

450ml Fish stock (page 301)
400g white fish fillets,
   skinned and cut into
   2cm pieces
200g cleaned scallops
400g raw prawns, peeled
50ml white wine
150ml whole milk
100ml double cream
50g butter
2 leeks, cut in half
   lengthways, washed
   and sliced
50g plain flour
Small handful flatleaf
   parsley, chopped
80g Emmental cheese,
   grated
50g panko breadcrumbs
Salt and black pepper

Caramelised apples
3 or 4 dessert apples
3 tbsp unsalted butter
2 tbsp golden caster sugar

Bring the stock to a simmer in a pan, then add the fish fillets and poach for one minute. Add the scallops and poach for another minute, then the prawns for a final minute. Remove them all with a slotted spoon and set aside. Add the wine, milk and cream to the stock and bring to the boil.

Melt the 50g of butter in another large pan, add the leeks and cook for about 5 minutes until soft. Add the flour and stir well, then add the milk and stock mixture, a ladleful at a time. Keep stirring until all the liquid is incorporated and the sauce is smooth with no lumps. Bring the sauce to the boil, turn down the heat and leave to simmer for about 15 minutes. Preheat the grill.

Grease 6 shallow ovenproof gratin dishes or one large dish measuring about 30 x 25cm. Add the poached fish, scallops and prawns to the pan and season with salt and pepper. Stir in the parsley, then transfer the mixture to the gratin dishes or dish. Mix the cheese with the breadcrumbs and sprinkle over the top. Place under the hot grill for 10 minutes until golden brown.

If you've made the gratin in advance and let it cool down, preheat the oven to 200°C/Fan 180°C and bake for 15–20 minutes until the top is brown and the filling is bubbling.

While the gratin is cooking, peel and core the apples and cut them into 2cm chunks. Melt the butter in a non-stick frying pan, then add the caster sugar and stir until the sugar has dissolved. Add the apple chunks and stir to coat them in the butter, then cook for about 10 minutes until the apples have softened and are covered in a caramel sauce. Serve the gratin with the caramelised apples on the side and some good bread.

You can also use cooked or frozen seafood, such as prawns, scallops and lobster, if you like. Just add them to the pan with the poached white fish.

Benjamin Bes and his father Denis have one of the beautifully ramshackle fishermen's sheds on the shore of the Étang de Gruissan in Languedoc-Roussillon. Many of the 30 or so cabanes also have a little stall where the fishermen sell their fish to the public, and most of them also have a simple brick barbecue for grilling their catch, mostly bass, gilthead bream and eels. There are two things that they say about the water of the étangs, a series of lagoons behind the seashore, in this part of the Languedoc. First, as the water is naturally saltier than the sea beyond, the fish have a sweeter flavour; and second, because trawlers are not allowed in, there are plenty of fish. What impressed me most, apart from the beautiful flavour of the fish, was the aïoli. I'm afraid I made a comparison with our British fishermen – would anyone back home consider making such a lovely sauce to go with their catch on the seaside? But the weather is a bit different. For me, aïoli is one of the absolute best sauces with fish and it does require a certain skill because of the ever-present danger of it splitting. Interestingly, they made their aïoli with sunflower oil, not olive oil. They said that olive oil was too strong and after tasting this I thought they had a point.

GRILLED BREAM WITH AÏOLI
DAURADE GRILLÉE À L'AÏOLI

SERVES 4

4 bream, gutted and
    cleaned but left whole
2 tbsp olive oil
Salt and black pepper

Aïoli
2–3 garlic cloves
2 egg yolks
½ tsp salt
1 tsp Dijon mustard
225ml sunflower oil

First make the aïoli. Pound the garlic in a pestle and mortar, add the egg yolks and season with salt and black pepper. Add the mustard, then gradually add the sunflower oil, pounding all the time until the mixture is a consistency that the pestle will stand up in. Alternatively, you can make this in a food processor like mayonnaise (page 302). Keep it in the fridge until ready to use.

Season the cavities and skin of the fish with salt, pepper and olive oil. Cook the fish on a barbecue or under a hot grill for about 5 minutes on each side. Serve with the aïoli and a simple green or tomato and fennel salad.

I wrote this recipe as a result of some irritation at being given such delicacies as perfectly fresh sardines in the fishing village of Port-Vendres that had been fried within an inch of their lives. It was almost like eating sticks. I'd noticed the same phenomenon after a morning's freshwater fishing on the Dordogne River. We had a lunch of hard-fried gudgeons, minnows, crayfish and eels, all overcooked in the same way; the saving grace was the mayonnaise. Granted a lot of river fish are quite tasteless but not sardines. No excuse there. Here's a better way. *Recipe photograph overleaf.*

GRILLED SARDINES WITH A TOMATO, GARLIC & THYME DRESSING

SERVES 4

12 sardines, cleaned
1 tbsp olive oil

Dressing
Juice and zest of ½ lemon
2 tbsp extra virgin olive oil
½ large clove garlic, grated
  or very finely chopped
¼ tsp piment d'Esplette
  (page 306) or a pinch
  of chilli flakes
1 medium tomato, skinned
  and cut into small dice
1 small shallot, finely chopped
1 thyme sprig,
  leaves chopped
1 tsp chopped flatleaf parsley
Salt and black pepper

Mix the ingredients for the dressing in a small bowl and season with salt and plenty of pepper.

Brush the sardines all over with the oil and sprinkle them with a pinch of salt. Grill them on a hot barbecue or under a hot grill for about 2–4 minutes on each side, depending on size.

Spoon the dressing over and around the sardines and serve with a green salad.

This is very much an autumnal dish making use of fresh ceps (porcini) and chestnuts and inspired by my early autumn visit to the Dordogne. I've had a lot of success partnering flatfish like brill or turbot with quite meaty sauces. It's a bit like putting curry with fish – some say curry spices completely mars the flavour but I always say as long as the fish is beautifully fresh, they enhance it. Some people don't approve of adding cheese to a fish dish, but I think a little salty, acidic, earthy Pecorino adds a sort of umami element to the sauce. You'll see that I've added some slow-cooked pig skin too which gives the sauce a lovely silkiness. You can leave this out, though, or use a little diced ham fat instead.

BRAISED FILLET OF BRILL WITH CEPS & CHESTNUTS
FILET DE BARBUE AUX CHAMPIGNONS ET MARRONS

SERVES 4

600ml Chicken stock (page 301)
700g brill, plaice or flounder fillets, skin on
100g unsalted butter
3 shallots, finely sliced
60g Confit pork skin, very finely diced (page 303), or diced ham fat
75ml dry white vermouth
100g vacuum-packed chestnuts, sliced
100g fresh ceps, sliced
2 tsp lemon juice
20g Pecorino Sardo cheese, finely grated
Small handful flatleaf parsley, chopped
Salt and black pepper

Pour the chicken stock into a wide pan and boil rapidly until it is reduced by half. Pour it into a jug and set aside.

Cut across each fillet so you have 4 pieces. Melt half the butter in a pan large enough to hold the fish fillets in one layer. Add the shallots and diced pig skin or ham fat and cook gently for 4–5 minutes. Add the vermouth, chestnuts and reduced chicken stock, then simmer for another 4–5 minutes until thickened. Add the ceps and lemon juice, and season with salt and pepper.

Place the fish fillets on top of the ceps, cover with a lid and cook for 6 minutes over a medium heat until the fish is cooked through. Carefully remove the fish and keep it warm. Add the remaining butter and the cheese to the pan and boil rapidly for a few minutes until the sauce coats the back of a spoon nicely. Stir in three-quarters of the parsley. Put the fish back in the pan and garnish with the rest of the parsley, then serve with buttery mashed potato and wilted spinach.

If ceps aren't in season, use large chestnut mushrooms with 20g of dried ceps. Reconstitute the dried ceps before using.

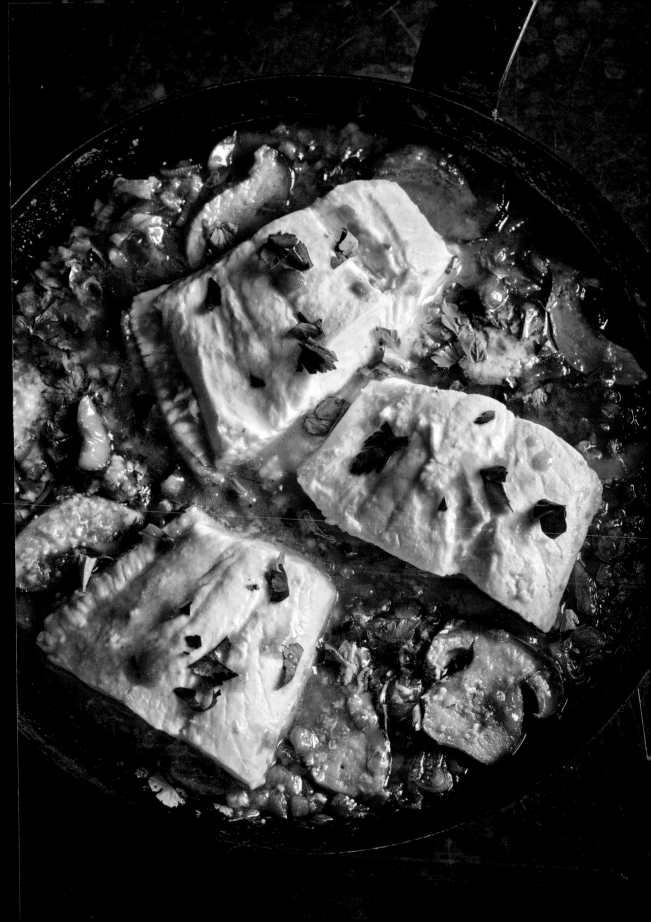

On my trip to Uzès, it had been arranged that a Dutch cook called Petra Carter, who has a popular cookery school in the town, was going to cook deep-fried courgette flowers stuffed with brandade for me. Sadly, though, she had slipped and broken her ankle so the cooking was off, but her friend Michelle Heuss, a very articulate Australian who runs food tours in Uzès, was available to take me to a fabulous shop there called La Maison de la Brandade. It's a branch of the most famous producer in nearby Nîmes – their brandade is called La Nîmoise. In addition to three styles of brandade, they sell pissaladière made with brandade and fougasse. But when I tasted the fragrance and delicacy of the brandade, the idea of using it to stuff courgette flowers was the one for me. Unfortunately, even with hot houses, courgette flowers have a very short season, so enjoy them while ye may! Now here's a bit of reality. When we tested this dish in the depths of winter, Portia and I had to find another way of containing the brandade and we used Chinese leaves. It produced something completely different but fabulous, and we decided to add a simple tomato dipping sauce to go alongside.

COURGETTE FLOWERS STUFFED WITH BRANDADE DE NIMES

SERVES 4

250g salt cod, soaked
   for 24 hours, water
   changed 3 times
2 cloves garlic,
   finely chopped
75ml double cream
75ml olive oil
8 courgette flowers or 8
   Chinese cabbage leaves
   (and 8 cocktail sticks)
Black pepper

Tomato dipping sauce
4 tomatoes
½ tsp piment d'Espelette
   (page 306) or pimentón
¼ tsp salt
Pinch sugar
1 tsp olive oil

Tempura batter
115g plain flour
115g cornflour
Pinch of salt
300ml very cold
   soda water
1 litre sunflower oil,
   for frying

Drain the cod, put it in a pan and add cold water just to cover. Bring to a simmer and poach for 5–10 minutes, depending on thickness. Remove the fish and leave it to cool. When it's cool enough to handle, flake the flesh, discarding any skin and bones.

Put the cod in a food processor with the garlic, cream and plenty of pepper. With the motor running, drizzle in the oil and process until you have a thick paste. Or, if you prefer, use a pestle and mortar. Put the paste in the fridge to chill for an hour.

To make the sauce, put the tomatoes, skin and all, in a blender with the piment d'Espelette, salt, sugar and oil, then whizz until fairly smooth. Pour into a small pan and cook for 2–3 minutes.

If using courgette flowers, stuff each flower with 2 tablespoons of the brandade paste and close the flowers around the stuffing. If using Chinese leaves, roll the leaf around the stuffing, tuck in the ends and secure with a cocktail stick.

Make the batter by sifting the flours into a bowl with the salt, then gradually whisk in the soda water. The mixture might be a bit lumpy, but that's fine.

Heat the oil in a large pan to 180°C. Dip the stuffed flowers or leaves into the batter, then carefully lower them into the hot oil, a few at a time. Fry for one minute until light and crispy, then remove and drain on kitchen paper. Carefully pull out the cocktail sticks, if used, and serve at once with the sauce.

I wouldn't say this is a particularly easy dish to perfect, coming as it does from a Michelin-starred chef called Tristan Arhan at Les Voiles d'Or, in Dieppe. The restaurant is on a headland above the harbour and looks out to sea past a slightly gloomy, dark church which is filled with sad plaques remembering the countless seafarers who have drowned over the years trying to bring in catches of beautiful fish to the famous Normandy port. This dish celebrates the John Dory and is perhaps most notable for its apparent simplicity. Just the fish, asparagus and mashed potato and a light sauce made with langoustine shells. When I ate it last May, everything was in season, including some wild asparagus which came with the cultivated, but I've had to make some changes to make the dish doable in the UK. I've added spinach in place of the wild asparagus, and made the langoustine emulsion with shell-on prawns. Finally, I've written the recipe for two people because it would be hard to get this all done and served warm for any more than that if you're cooking on your own. Tristan makes it for plenty more but then he's got a very well-equipped professional kitchen and chefs doing the prep. If you can't get John Dory, you could use cod, gurnard, or hake.

JOHN DORY WITH ASPARAGUS & PRAWNS

FILETS DE SAINT-PIERRE AUX ASPERGES ET CREVETTES

SERVES 2

2 x 175g John Dory fillets, skin on
10g butter, melted
350g potatoes, such as Desiree or Maris Pipers, cut into 5cm chunks
1 small garlic clove, chopped
3 tbsp olive oil
½ tbsp fresh oregano leaves, torn
80g fine asparagus spears, ends trimmed
100g spinach leaves, washed
100ml Shellfish reduction made with prawns (page 301)
25g cold unsalted butter, cut into small cubes
Squeeze of lemon juice
Salt and black pepper

Cut each fish fillet in half on the diagonal. Brush the fish and a small oven tray with the butter and sprinkle over some salt and pepper. Place the fish skin-side up on the tray and set aside.

Boil the potatoes in salted water, then drain and mash. Warm the garlic in the 2 tablespoons of the oil in a small pan, then beat this garlic-infused oil into the potatoes with the oregano leaves. Season and keep warm.

Steam or boil the asparagus for a couple of minutes until just tender. Blanch in cold water, drain and set aside. Heat the remaining tablespoon of oil in a frying pan, add the asparagus and fry briskly for 30 seconds. Season and keep it warm.

Put the spinach in a pan with the water that clings to the leaves. Wilt it over a gentle heat, then drain and keep it warm. Season with a pinch of salt.

Heat the shellfish reduction and whisk in the butter a cube at a time. Taste and season with salt and pepper and a squeeze of lemon juice.

Turn on the grill to high. Place the fish under the grill for 3–4 minutes until just cooked through and the skin has browned a little. Place some spinach on each warm plate, add neat spoonfuls of mash, then top with the fish, skin-side up. Add the asparagus, then finish by dotting the shellfish reduction over and around the dish.

These days, interviews about my books, television shows or anything else are normally covered by emails with lists of questions. I guess it's because, thanks to the internet, there are not that many journalists left any more. The questions range from such things as: Why did you decide to become a chef? Who is your favourite food personality? What would you whip up for a romantic candlelit dinner at home? Do you ever eat fast food? and inevitably a request for a quick recipe for fish. So the other day, almost as a defence, I thought through what would be my favourite quick fish dish and this is it. Amazingly, I then spoke to my chef friend Brian Turner who remembers going to Alain Passard's restaurant, L'Arpège, in Paris, where they ate red mullet and mayo and drank Puligny-Montrachet, so it's not just me who loves warm poached fish and mayonnaise.

POACHED RED MULLET WITH MAYONNAISE & TOMATO SALAD

SERVES 4

8 waxy new potatoes, skin on
1 mint sprig
2 tbsp double cream
4 tbsp Mustard mayonnaise (page 302)
4 red mullet (about 250g each), gutted and cleaned
2 tsp salt

Tomato salad
4 medium ripe tomatoes, peeled, at room temperature
½ tsp salt
1 tsp sunflower oil
½ tsp Rick's peppermix (page 303)
1 tbsp roughly chopped tarragon leaves

Scrub the potatoes and boil them in plenty of salted water with a sprig of mint until tender. Drain, cut them into quarters lengthways and keep them warm.

Mix the double cream with the mayonnaise to loosen the consistency a little and set aside.

Put the mullet in a large pan and barely cover with water. Add the salt and heat until the water is trembling and approaching a simmer. Immediately turn off the heat and leave the fish in the water. Using a temperature probe, check the thickest part of the fish and once it reaches 60°C, remove the fish and drain well. Peel back the skin and discard. Using a palette knife, lift the fillets whole from the bones (freeze the bones to use for fish stock).

For the salad, cut the tomatoes across into thin slices. Arrange these on a plate and just before serving sprinkle with half a teaspoon of salt and drizzle with the oil. Add a sprinkle of the peppermix and the chopped tarragon.

Serve the mullet with the new potatoes, mayonnaise and tomato salad.

I wouldn't say that my trip to France this time turned up any outstanding freshwater fish dishes. We went fishing on the Dordogne river and caught barbue, carp, bream, a fish called chevesne and rather a large catfish, not the sort of 130kg one that lives in holes in the mud but it was still 12–13kg. Afterwards we repaired to a restaurant in the village of Creysse, where we ordered freshwater crayfish, barbue, eel, catfish and minnows. I had really enjoyed messing about in the river, gliding into patches of water lilies, and yes, thinking about Jeremy Fisher. I quoted some Izaac Walton that runs as follows: 'Rivers and the inhabitants of the watery elements were made for wise men to contemplate and fools to pass by without consideration'. Indeed, I recalled that in the Beatrix Potter story, Jeremy invites his friends Sir Isaac Newton and Mr Alderman Ptolemy Tortoise for a lunch of roasted minnows. Ours were fried like everything else and served with rather indifferent aïoli. I decided to take the large catfish to Régis Ongaro, a well-known chef at a restaurant called La Belle Etoile in La Roque-Gageac, and I asked him to come up with a suitable local dish. He produced fishcakes containing much more than 50 per cent fish and subtly flavoured with lemon juice and piment d'Espelette. They were extremely good, made a lot thinner and wider than British ones, and served with this rocket salad, which I think is essential.

LA BELLE ETOILE FISHCAKES

SERVES 4

150ml milk
500g catfish or cod fillets
400g Maris Piper potatoes,
    cut into 3cm cubes
1 tsp piment d'Espelette
    (page 306) or pimentón
Juice of ½ lemon
½ tsp salt
50g plain flour
1 large egg, beaten
80g panko breadcrumbs
120g Clarified butter
    (page 303)
70g rocket leaves,
    washed and dried
1 tsp walnut oil
3 tsp balsamic vinegar

Bring the milk and 150ml of water to simmering point in a pan, then add the fish and poach for 8 minutes. Drain well and allow to cool slightly. Peel off the skin and discard it, then flake the fish, removing any bones as you go.

Boil the potatoes until tender, then drain them and allow to air dry in a colander. Mash them well and season with the piment d'Espelette or pimentón, lemon juice and salt. Mix with the fish. Shape into wide fishcakes about 2cm thick, then cover and chill in the fridge.

Preheat the oven to 180°C/Fan 160°C. Put the flour, egg and breadcrumbs in separate dishes. Coat each fishcake first in flour, then egg and finally breadcrumbs. Heat the clarified butter in a frying pan and fry the fishcakes for 5–6 minutes on each side until golden brown and crisp, then drain on kitchen paper. Finish them in the oven for 7–8 minutes.

Dress the rocket leaves with the walnut oil and balsamic vinegar and serve with the fishcakes.

Pascale Lefebvre's restaurant, L'Auberge de la Marine, is in Le Crotoy, on the eastern side of the Baie de Somme. He has a Michelin star for his excellent fish cookery and, as is de rigueur these days, the majority of his ingredients come from the area. For this dish, he uses spelt flour to coat thick fillets of pollack to get a nuttier flavour and a slightly coarser texture than with ordinary flour. What I liked about this dish is its simplicity – he's a man after my own heart. It goes without saying that the pollack needs to be of the first quality. Back home, I tested the dish with a couple of fillets landed at Newlyn Market that morning. Pollack needs to be absolutely fresh, otherwise its tantalising firm bite goes soft and flabby. Also, the fillets should be from a large fish, say four kilos plus. If in doubt, cod is an alternative.

POLLACK WITH MUSSEL & SAFFRON SAUCE

GOBERGE AUX MOULES SAFRANÉES

SERVES 2

5 tbsp olive oil
1 large banana shallot, finely chopped
75ml white wine
200g fresh mussels, scrubbed
1 or 2 fresh thyme, oregano or rosemary sprigs
200ml cold Fish stock (page 301)
50ml double cream
Pinch of saffron strands
2 x 200g pollack fillets, skin on
1 tbsp spelt or plain flour
30g butter
Salt and black pepper

Heat 2 tablespoons of the olive oil in a pan and cook the shallot over a medium heat until softened. Add the white wine, mussels, and herbs, then cover the pan. Once the mussels have opened, remove the pan from the heat and add the cold fish stock to stop the cooking. Drain the mussels in a sieve set over a bowl to catch the juices, then set them aside.

Pour the cooking liquid back into the pan and add the cream and saffron. Reduce by half and then simmer gently until the sauce coats the back of a spoon.

Heat the rest of the oil in a pan. Season the pollack fillets and dust them with flour. Fry the fish, skin-side down, then add the butter to the pan. Baste the fish with the foaming butter, then add the mussels to the pan to warm through.

Serve the fish, crispy skin-side up, with the mussels and sauce and some pommes purée (page 239) and green vegetables.

If you haven't been to the town of Uzès I would highly recommend it. It's one of those places where you find yourself surrounded by beautiful buildings and breathtaking squares, not to mention interesting and fashionable shops and restaurants. Of all the restaurants I visited in Uzès I particularly liked Restaurant Ten run by Kate Tucker and François Duplaix. Kate, who is English, seemed to have exactly the right professionalism and affection for the restaurant business, helped in no small way I guess by her time at the River Café in London. Continuing the connection with the UK, their most excellent chef, Damien Rolain, spent years working in great restaurants in Edinburgh. I have taken the liberty of simplifying his fabulous take on bouillabaisse, simply because there were too many stages for the home cook. *Recipe photograph overleaf.*

THE FLAVOURS OF BOUILLABAISSE WITH GURNARD & FENNEL

SERVES 4

5 tbsp olive oil
4–5 prawn shells or
   shell-on raw prawns
300g gurnard, filleted
   and cut into 6–7cm pieces
   (ask for the bones for stock)
1 fennel bulb, cut into thick
   slices, use stalk in the stock
½ tsp fennel seeds
2 strips of orange peel
2 shallots, chopped
3 garlic cloves, sliced
2 tomatoes, roughly chopped
1 tbsp tomato purée
½ tsp sugar
Pinch of saffron
150g monkfish tail
4 large raw shell-on
   prawns or langoustines
1 thyme sprig
1 tsp piment d'Espelette
   (page 306)
150g cooked small waxy
   potatoes, halved
4 tbsp tinned haricot beans,
   rinsed and drained
20 raw mussels
Salt

To serve
4 Confit tomatoes
   (page 225)
1 tbsp Green pistou
   (page 302)
Flaked sea salt

Start with the stock. Heat 3 tablespoons of the oil in a large pan, add the prawn shells or prawns, gurnard head and bones and fry for 10–15 minutes to caramelise.

Add the chopped fennel stalk, fennel seeds, orange peel, shallots, garlic, tomatoes, tomato purée, sugar and saffron to the pan and fry. Then add 800ml of water and half a teaspoon of salt and bring to the boil. Turn the heat down to a gentle simmer and cook for 45 minutes, uncovered.

Cut the monkfish tail into 4cm chunks and place them with the gurnard pieces, large prawns or langoustines and the thyme sprig on a baking tray. Drizzle with the remaining oil, then season with half a teaspoon of salt and the piment d'Espelette. Rub the oil and seasoning into the seafood and leave to marinate for 10 minutes.

Pulse the stock in a blender for about 15 seconds, then pass it through a fine sieve back into the rinsed pan. Add the fennel slices, cooked potatoes, haricot beans and mussels to the sieved stock and warm through over a gentle heat until the mussels have all opened.

Preheat the grill to high. Place the tray of marinated gurnard, monkfish and prawns or langoustines under the grill and cook for about 4 minutes. Add the grilled fish and shellfish to the hot stock and cook for a minute.

Serve in shallow bowls, making sure each serving has a large prawn or langoustine on top, and garnish with half a confit tomato. Drizzle over a little of the pistou and sprinkle with a few flakes of sea salt.

The Jura, with its steep limestone hills and honey-coloured buildings leading on to the Alpine landscape of the Haut-Jura, is utterly lovely, as anyone has been there will agree. How a region so close to Burgundy can be so overlooked at least by the British, I don't understand. Sometimes I wonder if it's the idiosyncrasy of Savagnin, the wine they make there, both in the grape and the method, that puts people off. It's a very yellow white wine which, because it's partly oxidised in the process of fermentation, comes out tasting a little like sherry; disconcerting if you're not in Andalucia. Also, because it's not fortified, Savagnin tastes like weak sherry. The things I've discovered about the wines of this region are that I do like a glass of cold Jura wine as an aperitif; the chardonnay they also make is full of character because it tastes slightly of Savagnin, and lastly Savagnin itself is a wonderful wine for cooking with. This recipe comes from the Le Relais des Abbesses guesthouse in the village of Château Chalon, where Sas and I stayed and which had a view right over Burgundy. The Vin Jaune gives the sauce a lovely yellow hue, but obviously you're not going to buy a bottle just for this – it costs about £30 – so unless you have a friend with some, use dry sherry instead.

SAUTÉED TROUT WITH SAVAGNIN

TRUITE SAUTÉE AU SAVAGNIN

SERVES 2

50g butter
1 shallot, finely chopped
60ml Savagnin wine
   or dry sherry
300ml Chicken stock
   (page 301)
100g full-fat crème fraiche
½ tsp Vin Jaune
   or dry sherry
1 tsp finely chopped parsley
Pinch salt
Pinch sugar
2 tbsp olive oil
4 trout fillets, each
   weighing about 75g

Heat 30g of the butter in a pan and sauté the shallot until softened. Add the Savagnin wine or dry sherry and the chicken stock, then reduce by about three-quarters. Whisk in the crème fraiche and reduce for a couple more minutes, then whisk in the remaining butter.

Continue to reduce until the sauce coats the back of a spoon, then remove the pan from the heat and add the Vin Jaune or dry sherry and the parsley. Season the sauce with salt and sugar and keep it warm.

Heat the oil in a large pan and cook the trout fillets, skin-side down, for about 4 minutes. Once the skin is golden, turn the fillets and finish cooking. Serve the fish with the warm sauce and some fine green beans or a green salad and new potatoes.

This recipe comes from the Hôtel Restaurant de la Place in Montmort-Lucy, just a little town we passed through on our journey south through Champagne. Most of us had this feuilletté for lunch. I loved it because it reminded me of things I ate on trips to France in the early 80s. Typically, a feuilletté consists of light puff pastry combined with hollandaise, sauce mousseline or a velouté and some form of seafood; scallops were very common. I guess the name feuilletté comes from millefeuille, thousands of leaves of pastry so crisp and light that they are, as the French often call them, like little clouds.

FEUILLETTÉ OF SMOKED SALMON & ASPARAGUS

SERVES 2
as a light lunch or brunch

About 175g all-butter
   puff pastry
1 egg, beaten
150ml Velouté sauce
   (page 302)
Lemon juice (optional)
10 young asparagus
   spears, ends trimmed
1 tsp white wine vinegar
2 eggs
100g smoked salmon, sliced
Salt and black pepper

Preheat the oven to 220°C/Fan 200°C. Roll out the pastry, cut out 4 x 10cm discs and place them on a baking tray. Lightly brush the pastry with beaten egg and bake for 8–10 minutes until golden and crisp. Set aside on a wire rack to cool.

Make the velouté sauce or reheat if made earlier. Season with salt and pepper and lemon juice if desired. Steam the asparagus until just tender and season with salt and pepper.

Bring a pan of water to a simmer and add the vinegar. Crack an egg into a cup. Stir the water to create a whirlpool, then gently add the egg to the water. Cook for about 3 minutes. Carefully remove the egg with a slotted spoon and drain briefly on kitchen paper. Repeat with the other egg.

Put a disc of puff pastry on each warm plate – keep the most attractive discs for the 'lids'. Top with slices of smoked salmon, then a poached egg. Spoon over a little of the sauce and cover with a puff pastry lid. Arrange the asparagus around the plate and spoon around the remaining sauce. Serve immediately.

This dish comes from a restaurant in Dieppe called Comptoir à Huîtres. I wished we'd filmed there, not only because it is a very good fish restaurant but also because it's in the industrial docks and across the road is a large complex full of off-shore windmill pieces; the juxtaposition of a really rather smart restaurant and industry works well on TV. This was a star dish for me, the fish just simply poached and served with a lovely vinaigrette of tomatoes, red onion, capers and parsley.

POACHED SKATE WITH A WARM TOMATO VINAIGRETTE

RAIE POCHÉE, VINAIGRETTE CHAUDES TOMATES

SERVES 2

2 x 225g skinned and
   trimmed skate wings
1 tbsp salt

Warm vinaigrette
5 tbsp extra virgin olive oil
½ tbsp red wine vinegar
½ small red onion,
   finely sliced
1 small tomato, skinned,
   seeded and finely chopped
1 tsp small capers, drained
½ tbsp finely chopped
   flatleaf parsley
Salt and black pepper

To poach the fish, bring 1.5 litres of water to the boil in a large shallow pan. Add the salt, then lower in the skate wings. Reduce the heat and simmer the fish for 10 minutes, until cooked.

Meanwhile, warm the olive oil, vinegar and red onion in a small pan. After a few minutes, turn off the heat and add the tomato, capers and chopped parsley and season with salt and pepper.

Serve the skate with the warm vinaigrette spooned over and some green beans on the side.

VOLAILLES

There is a giant metal sculpture of a chicken on the A39 eastern autoroute. It marks the services near the turn off to Bourg-en-Bresse, which is much like the Leigh Delamere services on the M4 in England but with a serious message about what's really special to eat in the region. All around are pastures full of plump white chickens. Locals speak patriotically of these birds, with their blue legs, white feathers and red combs, the bleu, blanc, rouge. Go into Bourg-en-Bresse and there's a surfeit of Bresse chicken on the menu in every restaurant. There are portraits of chickens in art galleries, and on key rings, postcards and fridge magnets in every newsagent. In the gift shop in the motorway services, they sell poulet de Bresse whole for the oven in distinctive red white and blue packaging for about 38 euros. Is this not France at its best? To pull in for petrol and leave not with a takeaway coffee, some wine gums or chocolate, but a great big Bresse chicken.

Needless to say the main fare in the services café is poulet de Bresse with buttered spinach and pomme frites. Never mind making a detour to a little country auberge; it's worth turning off at the Aire Poulet de Bresse just to have chicken for lunch.

In my opinion, buying a whole Bresse chicken to take home is worth every penny, though perhaps only once in a while. I first did so some time ago from a little shop in Rue du Pas de la Mule, just off the Place des Vosges in Paris. Even then it cost me about 22 quid. I took it back to Cornwall and we ate it roasted. Yes, you know I'll say it tasted like chicken used to taste, but what initially rather cast me down was that the flavour was almost too strong for me, at the time being all too used to supermarket chickens. These days my enthusiasm for the almost gamey flavour of proper free-range chicken has returned. And the stock I made that day from the bones was superb – almost a clear chicken soup.

All the chicken dishes in this chapter would be even better with a poulet de Bresse but none more so than the chicken fricassée with morels on page 150, traditionally made with this bird.

As for the duck recipes, I spent a couple of weeks in May cooking recipes from the book for the TV series. We were in a large, blue-shuttered stone house in the Luberon, near the peaceful town of Forcalquier, which was once the capital of Haute Provence. The house, set in remote countryside and surrounded by Mediterranean oaks and stretches of thyme and savory, was the sort of place where you could imagine writing *A Year in Provence*. Of all the dishes I cooked, the favourite was the duck cottage pie on page 174, but I think you're going to love the duck burgers on page 164 too.

I was very keen to go to Marseille on this trip. It's a fascinating city and would easily make it into my series of *Long Weekends* programmes. I have filmed there quite a bit in the past, mainly in the Vieux Port area, and particularly liked the little fish stalls there and the numerous places that advertise the best bouillabaisse, but I've always failed to pick up on the North African food, particularly from Tunisian restaurants. I developed a passion for couscous in the early 70s in Paris and to me, it's as satisfying as a curry. I remember the very first one I had: it arrived on a massive tray stuck with sparklers and it was called a couscous royale. Since then I've acquired a love of tagines too, after visiting Morocco a few times, so when I was at Le Palmier restaurant in Marseille I ordered both, though traditionally they're not supposed to go together. The tagine was chicken and fig, which sounded suitably exotic. After two months of French cuisine the spices were very welcome and I didn't mind that they don't serve beer.

CHICKEN & FIG TAGINE

SERVES 4–6

1 tsp ground ginger
1 tsp ground cinnamon
2 tsp ground cumin
2 tsp ground coriander
Pinch chilli flakes
Pinch ground allspice
8 chicken thighs, skin
   on and bone in
2 tbsp olive oil
1 onion, chopped
2 cloves garlic, chopped
150g ready-to-eat dried figs
Pinch saffron threads
500ml Chicken stock
   (page 301)
1 tbsp sesame seeds, toasted
30g flaked almonds,
   lightly toasted

Vegetable couscous
2 carrots
1 sweet potato
1 courgette
1 red pepper, seeded
30g butter
1 onion, sliced
1 tsp ras-el-hanout
5cm cinnamon stick
Pinch saffron
Pinch chilli flakes
750ml Chicken stock
½–1 tsp salt
250g couscous
Small handful fresh coriander
   leaves, roughly chopped

Mix the spices for the chicken in a bowl. Add the chicken thighs and rub the spices into them, then cover and refrigerate for at least 2 hours.

Heat a large tagine or casserole dish with a tablespoon of the oil. Brown the chicken pieces all over, then remove them from the pan. Add the remaining oil and fry the onion and garlic over a medium heat until softened but not browned. Put the chicken back in the pan and add the figs, saffron and chicken stock. Cover with a lid and cook over a low to medium heat for about 40 minutes. If there is too much liquid, continue to cook, uncovered, to reduce.

For the couscous, cut the vegetables into 3cm pieces. Melt the butter in a pan and fry the sliced onion with the spices for 4–5 minutes. Add the stock, salt and vegetables, bring to a simmer and cook for 20–25 minutes until the vegetables are tender. Drain and collect the stock in a jug. Keep the vegetables warm.

Put the couscous in a bowl and ladle some of the stock – about 500ml, depending on the couscous – over it. Cover and leave the couscous to stand for 5–10 minutes to swell up, then fluff with a fork. Spoon the vegetables over the couscous and add a little extra stock. Garnish with coriander.

Sprinkle the chicken tagine with toasted sesame seeds and almonds and serve it with the couscous.

For me, chicken with morels is as irresistible on a menu as turbot with hollandaise sauce. These days, I suppose people frown on a savoury dish with lots of cream in it, but the French invented this way of cooking and there is something so luscious and comforting about a beautiful free-range chicken cooked with a cream and wine sauce with the smoky flavour of dried morels. For me, this dish seems to be the very heart of French cuisine. It also happens to be a wonderful partner to a nice white Burgundy. There are variations of this dish. Traditionally it was made with poulet de Bresse and Savagnin, the Jura wine that has a slight sherry-like flavour. My preference is for Noilly Prat but sherry would be a good substitute. I don't think that sharper wines like Sauvignon or Riesling work because the cream element is crème fraiche and there is too much acidity in those wines.

CHICKEN FRICASSÉE WITH MORELS
FRICASSÉE DE POULET AUX MORILLES

SERVES 4

20g dried morels
200ml tepid water
40g unsalted butter
4 boneless chicken
    breasts, skin on
1 banana shallot,
    finely chopped
90g chestnut mushrooms,
    cleaned and quartered
100ml Noilly Prat
    (or dry sherry)
130ml Chicken stock
    (page 301)
300g full-fat crème fraiche
Salt and black pepper

Soak the morels in the tepid water for about 15 minutes, then drain them in a fine sieve over a bowl. Strain the liquid and reserve 75ml for the sauce. Rinse the morels under cold running water to remove any debris and dry them on kitchen paper. Cut them in half lengthways.

Melt half of the butter in a large sauté pan or frying pan. Fry the chicken, skin-side down, for 2–3 minutes until light golden brown, then turn them over and repeat on the other side. Take the chicken out of the pan and set aside.

Add the remaining butter to the pan. Fry the shallot over a medium heat until softened, then add the morels and chestnut mushrooms and fry for a few minutes. Add the Noilly Prat or sherry, the morel soaking liquid and chicken stock, bring to the boil, then turn the heat down and simmer for 2–3 minutes.

Add the crème fraiche and stir, then put the chicken back in the pan, along with any juices that have seeped out. Cover the pan and cook the chicken over a medium heat for about 8 minutes or until it is cooked through. Season with salt and plenty of black pepper and serve immediately with pilaf rice (page 303) or potatoes.

I had two reasons for going to Essoyes. First, because it's the centre of some of the best wines from Southern Champagne, notably Rémy Massin, which we visited and where we drank their Louis Aristide with salad. Second, Auguste Renoir lived there with his wife Aline who was from Essoyes, and the village is represented in many of his paintings. This reputedly was his wife's recipe for chicken sauté, which I really like. All versions of this dish are cooked in much the same way: you fry the chicken, deglaze the pan and add whatever flavouring ingredients you're using, then finish with a few delicate things such as mushrooms and Cognac, as here. What makes this dish really special is the addition of chicken livers, which are so finely chopped that they become more of a seasoning than an obvious flavour, and the final persillade – finely chopped garlic and parsley.

MADAME RENOIR'S CHICKEN SAUTÉ

SERVES 6-8

2 tbsp olive oil
1 free-range chicken, about
    1.75kg, jointed into 8 pieces
    (or use 8 good-sized
    chicken thighs, bone
    in and skin on)
30g unsalted butter
2 medium onions, sliced
1 large clove garlic, chopped
Handful flatleaf parsley,
    roughly chopped
A few thyme sprigs
1 bay leaf
2 large tomatoes,
    skinned and quartered
75g small button
    mushrooms, quartered
16 black olives, pitted
50g chicken livers, trimmed
    and finely chopped
2 tbsp Cognac
Salt and black pepper

Persillade, to serve
Handful flatleaf parsley
1 large garlic clove

Heat the oil in a shallow flameproof casserole dish or a frying pan and gently brown the chicken joints in batches. Set aside each batch as it is browned.

Add the butter to the pan and soften the onions, garlic and herbs. Season with salt and plenty of black pepper and add the tomatoes and 100ml of water. Put the chicken back in the pan and cook for 20-25 minutes. Check halfway through cooking and add a little more water if the dish looks dry.

Add the mushrooms, olives, chopped livers and the Cognac, then continue to cook for another 3-4 minutes.

Taste and season with more salt and pepper if needed and remove the thyme sprigs and bay leaf. Finely chop the parsley with the garlic and sprinkle over the dish, then serve at once with mashed potatoes and a green salad.

One of the highlights of my trip was going to the Restaurant du Fromage in Malbuisson in the Haut-Jura. I think there were eight courses, all containing prodigious amounts of cheese, lots of it naturally the local one – Comté. I have shamelessly written recipes for three of the courses: the tarte flambée on page 83, fondue on page 44 and this one. The family who run the place are doing very well because they also have a conventional restaurant, loads of hotel rooms and a lively bar, and – as almost always when a family are running a place, waiting, cooking and taking orders – the atmosphere is that bit special. The town of Malbuisson is well worth a visit. I am not familiar with Alpine places in the summer but, as a restaurateur, I'm quite envious of the fact that it was packed out in June and would presumably be crowded with skiers in winter; a double season. *Recipe photograph overleaf.*

CHICKEN LEGS STUFFED WITH MUSHROOMS & COMTÉ

SERVES 6

30g butter
2 tbsp olive oil
200g Portobello mushrooms, finely chopped
1 large clove garlic, finely chopped
75g cream cheese or mascarpone, beaten until soft
80g Comté cheese, finely grated
Small handful flatleaf parsley, chopped
1 tsp chopped fresh thyme leaves
6 chicken legs, bone in and skin on
Salt and black pepper

Heat 20g of the butter and a tablespoon of oil in a frying pan over a medium heat. Add the chopped mushrooms and garlic and fry for about 10 minutes until the mushrooms have given out their liquid and it has evaporated. Season with salt and pepper and set aside to cool.

Mix the cream cheese, Comté, parsley and thyme in a bowl, then stir in the cooled mushrooms. Season generously with salt and pepper.

Place a chicken leg skin-side down. Feel for the thigh bone with your fingers, then with a sharp knife carefully cut down through the flesh either side of the bone. With the tip of the knife, cut around the bone and scrape away the flesh, leaving the bone as clean as possible. Twist the bone at the joint with the drumstick and with scissors or a knife cut out the thigh bone, leaving the drumstick bone in place.

Fill the cavity left by the bone with a sixth of the mushroom stuffing. Using a few cocktail sticks, secure the chicken flesh around the stuffing. Brush the skin with the remaining olive oil, and season with salt and pepper. Repeat with the rest of the chicken legs.

Preheat the oven to 200°C/Fan 180°C. Brown the chicken legs with the remaining butter in a frying pan, then transfer to a roasting pan and roast for 25–30 minutes, or until the chicken is cooked through. Remove the cocktail sticks and serve with any juices from the roasting tin. Good with pommes purée with olive oil (page 239) and spinach.

I'm a bit of a late convert to big salads, the sort of things that people in Australia and California have been bringing along to parties in the sunshine for years. This salad is simply lots of great French ingredients, particularly the Carmargue red rice and the hot piment d'Espelette pepper. The trick is to get a good combination of textures – the slightly firm texture of the rice, the crispy ham, soft succulent poached chicken and a bit of crunch from the mangetout, all brought together with a classic vinaigrette dressing.

SALAD OF POACHED CHICKEN, RED RICE & PEACHES

SERVES 4
as a main course

2 skinless, boneless
   chicken breasts
2 tbsp olive oil
1 banana shallot,
   finely chopped
1 tsp piment d'Espelette
   (page 306) or pimentón
280g Carmargue red rice
1 tsp salt
Handful flatleaf parsley,
   roughly chopped
2 large ripe peaches,
   nectarines or figs, halved
1 tbsp runny honey
4 thin slices of Bayonne
   or Parma ham
150g mangetout, blanched
   and refreshed
2 tbsp pine nuts, toasted
4–6 tbsp Classic vinaigrette
   (page 302)
Salt and black pepper

Bring 700ml of water to a simmer in a wide pan. Add the chicken breasts and poach them for 10–12 minutes. Remove them and set them aside to cool, then slice on the diagonal. Reserve the liquid for cooking the rice.

In a large pan with a lid, heat the oil, add the shallot and piment d'Espelette and cook until softened. Add the red rice, 650ml of the hot chicken poaching liquid and a teaspoon of salt, then cover with the lid and turn the heat down to a simmer. Cook for about 30 minutes until the liquid has been absorbed and the rice is tender. Leave the rice to stand with a lid on the pan for a further 10–15 minutes. Stir in most of the chopped parsley.

Meanwhile, put the fruit on a piece of foil and drizzle it with the honey. Season the fruit with a little black pepper and grill it under a medium heat for 6–8 minutes until it's tender and brown around the edges. Set the fruit aside with its honey juices. Turn up the grill and grill the ham slices until crisp.

Spoon the red rice on to a large platter and scatter over the mangetout and grilled fruit. Add the sliced chicken, crisped ham, toasted pine nuts and remaining parsley, then drizzle the vinaigrette all over. Serve immediately.

Alsace's answer to coq au vin. The chef, food writer and designer Richard Cawley describes coq au vin as 'love in a lorry' and once you've heard that it slightly takes the romance out of this time-honoured French dish. In fact, I've never been entirely happy with coq au vin because the 'vin' bit always seems rather pale. I think if you are going to make a red wine sauce, make it deep and red, or everything can take on a rather mauve hue. Coq au Riesling, on the other hand works, much better because white wine with some cream and lots of parsley just looks much more appetising. The acidity of Riesling can be a rather surprising joy in Alsatian cookery.

COQ AU RIESLING

SERVES 4–6

2 tbsp vegetable oil
70g unsalted butter
12 shallots, peeled
    but left whole
3 cloves garlic,
    finely chopped
160g smoked bacon lardons
250g chestnut mushrooms,
    wiped and halved if large
1 free-range chicken
    (about 1.7kg), jointed
    into 8 pieces
1 tbsp plain flour
500ml medium-dry Riesling
350ml Chicken stock
    (page 301)
1 bay leaf
2 thyme sprigs
100ml single cream
1 egg yolk
Small handful flatleaf parsley,
    chopped, to garnish
Salt and black pepper

Heat half the oil and butter in a shallow flameproof casserole dish and fry the shallots, garlic and bacon lardons until the shallots have started to colour. Add the mushrooms and fry for a couple more minutes. Transfer everything to a bowl with a slotted spoon.

Add the remaining oil and butter to the casserole dish. Dust the chicken joints with flour and brown them in a couple of batches. Put all the chicken back in pan and add the wine, stock, herbs and the cooked shallots, lardons and mushrooms. Season with a teaspoon of salt and plenty of black pepper. Bring to a simmer and cook for about 20 minutes, uncovered. Pass everything through a colander set over a bowl and keep the chicken, lardons and vegetables warm.

Return the strained liquid and juices to the pan and reduce a little. Take the pan off the heat. Whisk the cream with the egg yolk and a ladleful of the reduced cooking liquid, then pour this into the pan with the stock. Place over a medium heat until the sauce has thickened, but don't let it boil.

Put everything back into the pan and let it warm through. Check the seasoning and garnish with chopped parsley. Serve with pommes purée (page 239) or buttered spätzle (page 187).

Something of a family staple all over France, poule au riz is one of those one-pot dishes that requires little thought but always turns out to be very nice. David Pritchard, the director I've worked with for over 30 years, maintained that Keith Floyd loved dishes like this, since you could start filming by browning off the chicken, then put the veg in the pot, add chicken stock, white wine, bay leaves and thyme, lid on, in the oven and go down to the pub for a couple. Come back, add the rice and cook for 20 minutes or so, then serve it up and a morning's filming would have been done. I need a little longer on Sunday, Wednesday and Friday evenings when I go to the pub. I arrive at seven, have two pints with my oldest friends and leave at ten to eight, but I find that this is a very cheerful dish to serve up after some less than riveting conversation about cars or rugby.

POULE AU RIZ

SERVES 6

1 tbsp oil
1 free-range chicken
   (about 2kg)
50g butter
250g shallots, peeled
   but left whole
250g carrots, chopped
   into 2cm pieces
6 celery sticks, trimmed
   and chopped into
   2cm pieces
2 leeks, cut in half
   lengthways, washed
   and sliced
6 cloves garlic, peeled
   but left whole
600ml Chicken stock
   (page 301)
200ml white wine
2 bay leaves
A few thyme sprigs
350g long-grain rice
Salt and black pepper

Preheat the oven to 150°C/Fan 130°C. Heat a large flameproof casserole dish, add the oil and brown the chicken all over. Take the chicken out, add the butter and when it's melted, add the shallots, carrots, celery, leeks and garlic and cook over a medium heat until softened.

Put the chicken on top and add the stock, white wine and herbs. Bring to the boil, season generously with salt and pepper, then cover with a tight-fitting lid and cook in the oven for 45–50 minutes. Add the rice to the juices around the chicken, cover and put the dish back in the oven for a further 20–25 minutes until the rice is tender and the juices have been absorbed.

Carve the chicken or cut it into joints and serve with the vegetables and rice.

Before the butcher in Padstow became a fudge shop (there's still a fish shop – mine!), Norman the butcher used to sell chickens cooked in a rotisserie and very generously he used to give me the cold fat and chicken juice that dripped down into the trough under the roasting chickens. I can honestly say I've never tasted a better glace de viande and I used it to enliven many a sauce, even fish-based ones. In France, particularly in Provence, they craftily put sliced potatoes underneath a roasting chicken, which produces an unforgettable sort of pommes boulangère. Sometimes they season it just with salt and pepper, sometimes they add spices and also onions, garlic and red peppers. Whichever way, this is simply chicken, slow-roasted in the oven with the vegetables underneath. *Recipe photograph overleaf.*

ROTISSERIE-STYLE CHICKEN

SERVES 4–6

½ lemon
1 clove garlic, bashed
1 free-range chicken
 (about 1.7 kg)
600g potatoes, cut
 into 2cm thick slices
2 tbsp olive oil

Spice rub
2 tsp paprika
Good pinch cayenne
1 tsp salt
½ tsp dried thyme
40g butter, softened

Preheat the oven to 150°C/Fan 130°C. Put the lemon half and the garlic in the cavity of the chicken, then tie the legs together with cooking string.

Mix the rub spices and seasonings together and blend them with the butter. Smother the seasoned butter all over the chicken.

Place the chicken on a bed of potatoes in a roasting tin and surround it with the remaining potatoes. Drizzle the olive oil over the potatoes and then roast for 2–2½ hours. Baste the chicken and potatoes a few times during the cooking time. Serve immediately with the pan juices spooned over.

This recipe comes from the village of Trémolat in the Dordogne. My reason for going there was not gastronomic but because it was the location of a favourite film of mine, *Le Boucher* starring Stéphane Audran; the director was her husband Claude Chabrol. It's a dark tale of a butcher who served in the Algerian war and became a killer as a result of his experiences. I hadn't done my research but I soon realised there's a fabulous Relais et Châteaux hotel in Trémolat called Le Vieux Logis, where Chabrol and his wife stayed while filming. The rooms, the one-Michelin-star restaurant and the gardens are delightful, and they also have a bistro and a café in the village. The café, Tartine, serves these delicious duck burgers which are a real step up from your average high street burger. Lovely with matchstick potatoes.

DUCK BURGERS

SERVES 4

800g duck meat
    (breast, leg or a mixture)
½ tsp salt
1 tsp Rick's peppermix
    (page 303)
Oil, for greasing
80g cheese such as
    Comté or Gruyère,
    cut into 4 slices
4 brioche or burger
    buns, halved
2–3 tsp grainy mustard
Large handful rocket leaves
1 tsp walnut oil
1 small onion, finely sliced
1 dill pickle, sliced
1 large tomato, sliced
2 tbsp Mustard mayonnaise
    (page 302)

Matchstick potatoes
450g floury potatoes,
    such as Maris Pipers
Sunflower oil, for deep-frying

Pull the fat off the duck and mince 100–150g of it with the meat and skin. Save the rest of the fat for another dish. Season with the salt and peppermix. With slightly damp hands, form the mixture into 4 patties. Flatten them a little, then cover and leave them in the fridge for an hour or so to firm up.

For the matchstick potatoes, cut the potatoes into short sticks, about 3mm thick, by hand, or use a mandolin. Set them aside in a bowl of cold water. Heat the oil in a large pan to 190°C. Drain the potatoes and dry them well. Plunge them into the hot oil and fry for 3 minutes, until crisp and golden. Drain on kitchen paper and keep them warm in a low oven.

Lightly oil a ridged or flat griddle pan or a non-stick frying pan and place it over a high heat. When it's hot, cook the burgers for 3–4 minutes on each side. Add a slice of cheese to the top of each burger, turn off the heat and allow them to sit for a minute or so while the cheese starts to melt. You can also cook these burgers on a barbecue.

Lightly toast the buns and spread the cut surfaces of each bun with mustard. Dress the rocket leaves with the walnut oil.

Make up the burgers with sliced onion, dill pickle, tomato, mayo and rocket, then serve with the matchstick potatoes.

Arriving at Lucy and Pinky Image's home at Allemans in the Dordogne is a bit like experiencing the house in *A Year in Provence* with a dash of the *Darling Buds of May*. Without any suggestion of criticism I would call the place gorgeously ramshackle. The garden is a little overgrown and over most of the house is a grapevine from which they make a passable red wine. There's a big al fresco dining area, flowers everywhere, fig trees – you name it it's all there. I was a bit disconcerted by Lucy's suggestion of making a North African duck fatteh, but reasoned that it would fit here because there is such a connection between France and North Africa. With its combination of duck confit and Middle Eastern flavours, it reminded me of the sort of thing you'd get in California, where they have no qualms about mixing cuisines. This may seem quite a bit of work but remember, you're serving lots of people with one dish and much of it can be made in advance.

FATTEH SALAD WITH CONFIT DUCK

SERVES 8–10

1 aubergine
1 tbsp olive oil
2 large garlic cloves
8 firm plums, halved
   and stoned
1 tbsp soft brown sugar
2 x 5cm cinnamon sticks
2 star anise
4 or 5 cloves
3 Confit duck legs
   (page 303 or bought)
200g full-fat crème fraiche
Salt and black pepper

Rice
30g butter
2 tbsp olive oil
2 onions, finely sliced
600g long-grain or basmati
   rice, rinsed and drained
800ml Vegetable stock
   (page 301) or water
400g tin chickpeas,
   drained and rinsed
8cm cinnamon stick

To serve
8 tbsp Tomato sauce
   (page 302 or bought)
4 flatbreads
Walnut halves,
   lightly toasted
Handful flatleaf
   parsley, chopped

Preheat the oven to 200°C/Fan 180°C. Cut the aubergine into rough 4cm chunks. Put them in a roasting tin, toss them with the oil and sprinkle with a little salt. Add the garlic to the tin and roast everything for 25 minutes until tender, then set aside.

Reduce the oven temperature to 140°C/Fan 120°C. Place the plum halves in an ovenproof dish, sprinkle them with sugar and add the whole spices. Lay the duck legs on top, with just the fat that clings to them – keep any excess fat for another dish – and bake for one hour. Remove from the oven and keep warm. Remove the garlic flesh from roasted cloves and mash it into a paste. Stir this into the crème fraiche and season with a good pinch of salt. Set aside.

For the rice, melt the butter and oil in a large shallow pan that has a lid. Sweat the onions over a low to medium heat for 5–10 minutes until soft but not coloured. Add the rice and stir to coat it all in the buttery onions, then add the stock or water, chickpeas and cinnamon stick. Cover the pan and simmer for 15–20 minutes, then remove the lid and fluff up the rice with a fork. Season with salt and pepper.

Transfer the rice and chickpea mixture to a serving dish. Slice or shred the duck and place it on top. Discard the whole spices from the plums and add them with their juice. Add the aubergines, dot over the tomato sauce, then the garlic crème fraiche. Toast the flatbreads and cut them into triangles. Garnish the dish with walnuts and parsley and add the flatbreads. Serve with a salad.

I like to make this with Islay malt whisky because it gives a slight smoky flavour, but the correct spirit is Cognac, which is lovely too. The classic accompaniment to duck liver parfait should be Château d'Yquem or any other delicious Sauternes, but the partnership between the pâté and fig relish, which is made more like a confit with lemon juice, rather than a jam or a highly vinegered chutney, works a treat. Melba toast is a must with this.

DUCK LIVER PARFAIT WITH FIG 'RELISH'

MAKES ONE TERRINE

450g duck livers, trimmed
   of any white sinew
1 small shallot, chopped
1 clove garlic, chopped
2 tbsp port or sweet sherry
1 tbsp Islay malt whisky
   or Cognac
40ml double cream
1 tsp salt
½ white pepper
225g unsalted butter,
   melted and cooled
   slightly, plus extra
   for greasing

To seal
100ml Clarified butter
   (page 303)

Fig relish
8 large fresh figs,
   325–350g, stems
   removed, quartered
100g soft brown sugar
1 tbsp lemon juice
Generous pinch dried
   chilli flakes
5cm cinnamon stick
½ tsp salt

To serve
Melba toast (page 303)

For the fig relish, put all the ingredients in a pan, place over a medium heat and stir regularly to allow the sugar to dissolve. Bring to a simmer and cook for 15–20 minutes until the figs have softened and the mixture is deep pink and jammy.

Decant into sterilised jars and allow to cool. This will keep for a few weeks in the fridge and is also delicious with cheese.

Preheat the oven to 110°C/Fan 90°C. Line a 450g loaf tin with cooking-grade cling film. Put the duck livers, shallot, garlic, port or sherry, whisky or Cognac and the cream into a food processor and add the salt and white pepper. Blend for one minute until smooth. Add the cooled melted butter and blend for a few seconds, then press the mixture through a fine sieve into a bowl.

Transfer the mixture to the lined tin and cover with a sheet of lightly buttered foil. Place the loaf tin in a roasting tin half filled with hot water. Transfer to the oven and cook for 1¼ hours, then remove and leave to cool.

Take off the foil, melt the clarified butter and pour it over the top. Leave to chill for at least 4 hours, then serve with fig relish and melba toast.

Tom Kevill-Davis wrote a book called *The Hungry Cyclist* and he's married to Aude Bonnetain, whose family make excellent Burgundy in Auxey-Duresses. In his book, this is what he had to say about grape picking. 'For all its "bucolic romance" picking grapes in Burgundy is back-breaking work. Seemingly endless days are spent bent-double, snipping at grapes while you steadily hike uphill. The work is relentless and monotonous and the high point of each day is lunch. Served at a communal table back at the domain, this is a moment to drink, recharge and refill. Four courses are served generously and washed down with unprofessional amounts of wine, before everyone staggers back into the vineyards for the arduous afternoon shift. As well as working in the vines herself, day after day, Aude's mother miraculously rolls out faultless four-course feasts for the 20-strong team of dog-tired workers slumped around her table. Her food is exceptional and a standout dish among the loyal workers, who return year after year, is parmentier de confit de canard. Unctuous, filling and restorative, it has legendary status among the team.'

DUCK COTTAGE PIE
PARMENTIER DE CONFIT DE CANARD

SERVES 4–6

4 Confit duck legs
  (page 303 or bought)
4 shallots, chopped
A few fresh thyme sprigs,
  leaves stripped and
  chopped
175ml red wine
200ml Chicken stock
  (page 301)
Handful flatleaf parsley,
  chopped
800g potatoes,
  cut into 5cm chunks
100–125ml warm milk
150–200g Comté
  cheese, grated
Salt and Rick's peppermix
  (page 303) or black
  pepper

Warm the confit duck legs over a gentle heat to release the fat, then pour the fat into clean jam jars. You will need some for this dish, but save the rest for roasting potatoes another day.

Remove the skin from the duck legs and discard it or slice and roast as a nibble. Pull away the duck meat with a couple of forks and shred it, removing and discarding any bones and gristle.

Heat 2 tablespoons of the duck fat in a pan, add the shallots, thyme and half a teaspoon of peppermix or plenty of black pepper. Allow the shallots to brown gently and once they are golden, add the wine and stock, then bring to the boil. Cook for a few minutes, then add the duck meat and the chopped parsley. Stir and set aside.

Preheat the oven to 210°C/Fan 190°C. Boil the potatoes in salted water for 20–25 minutes until tender. Drain them well, then add the warm milk and mash until smooth. Season with salt and a big pinch of peppermix or some black pepper.

Grease a baking dish measuring about 18 x 28cm with duck fat. Pile in the meat mixture, then cover with mashed potatoes. Sprinkle the grated cheese on top and bake for about 25 minutes until heated through and browned on top.

Serve with a green salad, green beans with garlic and fried breadcrumbs (page 230) or carrots à la fermière (page 250).

It would be wrong not to admit that on every trip I make in my food and travel journeys there are always some favourite places, ones that seem to sum up the essence of a country for me. In France this time, it was that part of Burgundy around Charolles, famous for its cattle. It couldn't have been a better time of year because at dawn in early June I could smell the grass through the open windows of the château I was staying in, and looking out at a view of complete greenery over the gently upward-sloping pastures, dotted with oak trees and the white stumpy cattle up to their knees in the lush grass, I had an epiphany of what French agriculture means; it is absolutely the heart of the country.

Later that morning at the cattle market, le marché aux bestiaux, at Saint-Christophe-en-Brionnais, I wandered through the yards splattered with cow shit that smelled, as I remarked at the time, of sweet grass, looking at this sturdy breed. They have broad shoulders, big heads and large muscles, and they produce, I have to admit, the most succulent of steak.

Charolais beef, I was told by the market director Antoine Gronfier, has suffered in reputation because of the ease with which it can be reared virtually anywhere in the world, and also because with those big limbs the cattle have a very high meat yield. Breeds like Longhorn, Devon, Aberdeen Angus and Welsh Black are held in higher esteem, but Charolais cattle from the region that feed on grass from the local pastures are a different matter. In fact, as with so much special produce in France, they carry an appellation contrôlée, the main requirement of which is that they have to be fed exclusively on the lush local grass, including hay made from the same grass out of season.

Unashamedly, I've loaded this chapter with beef – fillet steak, onglet, braised short ribs, beef stews – not just because I love it but because it's always a good reason for ordering red wine. So much of French cooking is almost an excuse for a glass. I don't believe anywhere in the world understands the partnership better, and in Burgundy with a simple plate of very rare steak it would have to be a local red wine, not an expensive one but a two to five-year-old Côte Chalonnaise like Rully, Mercurey or Montagny.

I bought a couple of jars of enchaud Périgordin in Périgueux market. It's pork loin studded with garlic and pot-roasted with a small amount of stock and pig's trotters, then left to go cold before being bottled. It's designed to be thinly sliced and served with other cold meats, pâtés and pickles. I found it delicious but a little on the dry side, and several attempts to reproduce the dish ended in frustration as being loin, the meat ended up dry. I decided therefore to create a version in which I stud the pork loin with plenty of garlic in the same way, wrap it in the skin to keep in the moisture and pot-roast it with lots of root vegetables for a deep winter flavour. I serve it thinly sliced with the vegetables and strained juices.

POT-ROAST PORK
ENCHAUD PÉRIGORDIN

SERVES 6

1kg boned pork loin
2 cloves garlic
50g salted butter
300g each of swede,
    carrot, onion, cut
    into 3cm chunks
500ml Beef or Chicken
    stock (page 301)
A few thyme sprigs
2 bay leaves
½ tsp Rick's peppermix
    (page 303)
Salt

Ask your butcher to remove the skin from the pork loin, leaving about 1cm of fat on the meat. You will need the skin as well.

Slice the garlic into slivers, cut evenly spaced holes in the meat with the tip of a small knife and insert a garlic sliver into each one. Lay the pork on the reserved skin, roll it up and tie it with butchers' string to hold it in place – the skin will keep the meat moist. Cover and leave it in the fridge for at least 4 hours.

Preheat the oven to 180°C/Fan 160°C. Melt the butter in a flameproof casserole dish over a medium heat, add the pork and brown it well on all sides. Remove the pork, then add the vegetables and fry until lightly browned. Put the pork back in the pan on top of the vegetables.

Pour the stock over the pork, add the thyme and bay leaves and season with the peppermix and some salt. Cover with a tight-fitting lid and cook in the oven for 1¼ hours. Check with a meat thermometer if you have one; the internal temperature of the meat at the end of the cooking time should be 70°C.

Put the meat on a board, remove the string and the skin and set aside, then cover the meat with foil to keep it warm. Preheat the grill to medium and put the grill pan on the lowest rung. Sprinkle the skin with salt and grill it until crisp.

Transfer the vegetables to a serving dish with a slotted spoon and keep them warm. Spoon off any excess fat from the juices in the pan, then pass the juices through a sieve and pour them into a warm jug. Taste and adjust the seasoning if necessary. Carve the pork into thin slices and serve with the vegetables, crispy skin and juices.

This is one of those recipes that seems to have been around forever, with good reason, and this is my version of it. The reason it works so well is the combination of lean pork, cream and sweet prunes, given an aromatic edge by brandy – preferably Cognac or Armagnac. It's a classic à la minute restaurant dish – it's prepared and cooked when you order it.

MEDALLIONS OF PORK WITH PRUNES & COGNAC

SERVES 4

30g butter
2 tsp vegetable oil
700g pork fillet, trimmed
    of silvery sinew and
    cut into 1cm rounds
2 banana shallots, chopped
60ml Cognac or brandy
150ml double cream
250ml Chicken stock
    (page 301)
2 tsp redcurrant jelly
A few fresh thyme sprigs
12 ready-to-eat pitted prunes
Small handful flatleaf parsley,
    roughly chopped
Salt and black pepper

Heat half the butter with the oil in a frying pan and brown the pieces of pork for 1-2 minutes, then set them aside.

Add the remaining butter and the shallots and cook until softened. Then add the Cognac or brandy and cook for a minute or so until the liquid is reduced by half.

Add the cream, chicken stock, redcurrant jelly, thyme sprigs and prunes and cook for a couple of minutes before putting the pork slices and any juices back in the pan. Taste and season with salt and plenty of pepper, then cook for 3-4 minutes until the pork is cooked through. Remove the thyme and sprinkle over the parsley.

Serve with pommes purée (page 239) and some spinach or buttered cabbage.

Le Saint Eutrope restaurant is near the black Gothic cathedral in Clermont-Ferrand, for me, one of France's best-kept secrets. The city is largely built out of volcanic rock, hence the cathedral, and it's famed for being the HQ of the Michelin tyre company yet is bustling with clubs, bars, interesting restaurants and students. The restaurant is run by Harry Lester and his wife Alexandra and I suspect they chose the city because it seems like anything is possible there. I really liked the place, partly because it reminded me of my own restaurant when I started out – a menu that changes every day, furniture and décor a bit mismatched, kitchen a bit too small – and Harry, though overworked, is definitely nailing it. The crew and I ate this dish on a Sunday lunchtime, sitting outside in a narrow street called Rue Saint Eutrope. I love deep-fried breadcrumbed pork chops, it's something we don't really do in the UK. Harry served the chops with fried parsley, and braised peas seemed a perfect accompaniment. His wine list is extraordinary; he has lots of chums making whacky vintages in weird parts of France. *Recipe photograph overleaf.*

DEEP-FRIED PORK CHOPS WITH PARSLEY

SERVES 4

4 x 175–200g bone-in
  pork chops
50g plain flour
1 large egg, beaten
100–120g panko breadcrumbs
500–750ml vegetable oil
Small handful flatleaf parsley
  leaves, very well dried
lemon wedges (optional)
Salt and black pepper

Season the pork chops well with salt and pepper. Put the flour, beaten egg and breadcrumbs in separate wide bowls. Dip each seasoned chop in flour, then egg and finally breadcrumbs, making sure each has a fairly thick coating of crumbs.

Pour the oil into a large pan – the exact amount will depend on the size of your pan but it should be about 5cm deep. Heat the oil to 160–170°C. Don't try to cook all the chops at once or they won't brown. Deep-fry them, 2 at a time, for about 3–4 minutes on each side, depending on thickness, until deep golden brown. The internal temperature should be 71°C. Drain the fried chops on a triple layer of kitchen paper, then keep them warm in a low oven while you cook the rest.

Once the chops are cooked, quickly deep-fry the parsley leaves. Serve the chops, garnished with the parsley, right away while they are hot and crisp, with lemon wedges if you like and some braised peas (page 234) on the side.

This comes from a restaurant called La Cocotte Rouge in the hills above Kaysersberg in Alsace. It's owned by Christophe Frey and his family, who also have a game butchery and deli in the village of Fréland, and in addition to cuts of various species of deer and wild boar they do sausages, hams and pies. Next door to the shop, they have an art gallery which features lots of food paintings of fabulous eccentricity, some of them not at all appetising. Christophe calls the whole enterprise his 'Art Boucherie'. This stew is quite simple and designed to bring out the best in a glass or two of Alsace Pinot Noir. Start the preparations the day before.

WILD BOAR STEW WITH PINOT NOIR

CIVET DE SANGLIER AU PINOT NOIR

SERVES 4–5

1kg wild boar shoulder,
  cut into 4cm cubes
750ml Pinot Noir
2 carrots, sliced
1 onion, chopped
1 onion, studded
  with 8 cloves
4 tbsp sunflower oil
2 cloves garlic, chopped
400ml Beef stock
  (page 301)
1 Bouquet garni
  (page 303)
1 1/2 tsp salt
1/2 tsp Rick's peppermix
  (page 303)
2 tbsp Beurre manié
  (page 303)

Persillade
Handful flatleaf parsley
1 large garlic clove

Put the cubes of wild boar in a large non-metallic bowl with half the wine, the carrots, chopped onion and whole studded onion. Cover and leave to marinate in the fridge for 24 hours. The following day, strain the meat and vegetables well in a colander over a bowl to collect all the marinade juices.

Heat 2 tablespoons of the oil in a large heavy frying pan and fry the meat over a medium heat. Work in batches so you don't overcrowd the pan and turn the meat to ensure all sides are nicely browned.

Once all the meat is browned, set it aside and brown the carrots, chopped onion and garlic. Put all the meat and vegetables in a casserole dish and add the studded onion, the marinade juices, the remaining red wine, the stock and bouquet garni, then season with the salt and peppermix. Bring everything to the boil and then turn down to a simmer and cook for 1 3/4–2 hours or until the meat is very tender.

Pour the contents of the pan into a colander set over a bowl to collect the strained juices. Discard the bouquet garni and the studded onion. Pour the juices back into the pan, then boil until reduced to intensify the flavour.

Whisk in as much of the beurre manié as needed to thicken the sauce. Put the meat and vegetables back in the pan and coat with the glossy sauce. Sprinkle with the persillade, then serve with spätzle (opposite) or some mashed potatoes.

A wild boar stew would be nothing without the accompaniment of spätzle. Like so many dishes in Alsace, the orgins of this are as much German as French or Swiss.

SPÄTZLE

SERVES 2–4

250g plain flour
1 tsp salt
2 eggs, beaten
125ml milk
40g butter
A few rasps freshly
    grated nutmeg
Black pepper

Sift the flour and salt into a bowl. Make a well in the centre, add the eggs and whisk them into the flour. Keep whisking and gradually add the milk until you have a thick batter. Cover and leave to rest in the fridge for about 30 minutes.

Bring a large pan of salted water to the boil, then turn the heat down to a simmer. Rest a colander over the pan, ensuring it is not touching the water. Add the batter to the colander and push the mixture through the holes with a plastic spatula. Cook for 2–3 minutes or until all the 'noodles' have risen to the surface. Drain well.

Heat the butter in a frying pan and when it is foaming toss in the spätzle and fry until golden and coated in the butter. Rasp over the nutmeg, stir well and remove from the heat. Season with black pepper and more salt if required.

Spätzle can also be served as a main dish. Put the 'noodles' in a baking dish, top with fried onions and grated Gruyère and bake for about 20 minutes at 200°C/Fan 180°C.

One notable difference between France and Britain is the absence of 'foreign' restaurants, apart from in major cities such as Paris, Bordeaux or Lyon. You might find the odd Vietnamese or North African establishment but to discover a Japanese restaurant in a relatively industrial city like Clermont-Ferrand was unusual. It was in a little side street across from our hotel and we went there twice because it was so good. I couldn't help thinking that if David Pritchard, the director I worked with for nigh on 30 years, was still with us we would have filmed in this tiny restaurant, even though the series is about French cooking. It's been run by just one Japanese man for the last 40 years and the only other staff appeared to be a girl who came in for a few hours on Saturdays. But his sashimi was exquisite, only salmon, and his katsudon was the best I've ever tasted.

KATSUDON

SERVES 2

200g Japanese
   short-grain rice
2 x 100–120g pork
   loin steaks
50ml vegetable oil,
   plus 1 tbsp
½ onion, finely sliced
150ml dashi stock
   (see suppliers, page 309)
2 tbsp Japanese soy
   sauce, plus extra
   to serve
1 tbsp mirin
1 tsp caster sugar
2 eggs, beaten
2 spring onions,
   trimmed and sliced
   on the diagonal
Salt and black pepper

For coating the pork
40g plain flour
1 egg, beaten
40g panko breadcrumbs

Wash the rice in a bowl, using plenty of changes of water until the water runs clear. Leave to soak for 30 minutes, then drain. Put the rice in a pan with 250ml of water, cover and bring to the boil, then simmer for 10 minutes. Turn off the heat and leave the rice covered for another 10 minutes.

Season the pork with a little salt and pepper. Put the flour, beaten egg and breadcrumbs in separate wide dishes. Dip each steak in flour, then egg and finally breadcrumbs.

Heat the 50ml of oil in a frying pan. Fry the pork steaks for 4–5 minutes on each side, then cut them into finger-width slices.

Wipe out the frying pan. Add the tablespoon of oil to the pan and gently fry the onion for a couple of minutes until soft. Add the dashi, soy sauce, mirin and caster sugar and bring to a simmer, then place the slices of pork in the pan. Heat them through for a minute or two, then add the beaten eggs around each steak and allow them to cook. Add the sliced spring onions over and around the pork and eggs.

Fluff up the rice and divide it between two bowls. Top each serving with a pork steak and the egg, onion, stock mixture. Serve at once with more soy sauce at the table if you like.

Choucroute garnie is reason enough to travel to Alsace. With the sour aromatic cabbage, smoked meat and boiled potatoes, it's one of those combinations that makes perfect food for animated conversation. In other words, it's lovely, but I don't need to talk about it. It also has the inestimable quality of feeling healthy, simply because sauerkraut and other fermented vegetables have had almost immortal qualities attributed to them. The harvesting of the cabbage goes from the beginning of July to the end of September, and incidently the main village where it is grown is called Krautergersheim, which means 'the place of cabbage'. The meats most commonly served in choucroute are smoked pork, pork neck, Strasbourg sausage, Montbéliarde sausage and boudin blanc. Boudin noir and coarse chopped liver are added to the royale version, but I have rationalised the meat for us mere mortals.

CHOUCROUTE ALSACIENNE

SERVES 4

900g sauerkraut, finely cut
1 clove garlic, crushed
    or grated
2 tbsp lard or duck
    or goose fat
1 onion, finely chopped
10 juniper berries
2 bay leaves
¼ tsp cloves
1 tsp cumin seeds
1 tsp mustard seeds
675ml Riesling white wine
1.5 litres Chicken stock
    (page 301)
8 waxy new potatoes, peeled
320g piece of unsmoked
    streaky bacon, sliced into 4
4 good-quality frankfurter/
    Bockwurst sausages
    (see suppliers, page 309)
200g Montbéliarde sausage
    or smoked Polish sausage
    (see suppliers, page 309),
    cut into 5–6cm lengths
250g smoked pork loin,
    cut into 5cm chunks
Salt and black pepper

Put the sauerkraut into a large pan or stockpot with the garlic, lard or duck or goose fat, onion, juniper berries, bay leaves, cloves, cumin seeds, mustard seeds and wine. Add 150ml of water, cover with a lid and cook for about 2 hours over a low to medium heat. Season with salt and plenty of pepper.

In a separate pan heat the stock to boiling point. Reduce the heat to a simmer, add the potatoes and slices of bacon, then cook for 20 minutes. Add the frankfurters, Montbéliarde or Polish sausage and the smoked pork loin and cook for 10–12 minutes. Drain the meat and potatoes, discarding the stock.

To assemble, drain the sauerkraut in a fine sieve, pushing it down to squeeze out any excess liquid. Turn it out on to a serving dish. Arrange the pork, sausages and potatoes around the sauerkraut and serve immediately with mustard.

Le Crotoy in the Somme is not that well known to us and it's a bit of a find, particularly the Hôtel Restaurant les Tourelles which in former times was much used by the Guerlain family, who had a substantial house nearby. I like to think that the fragrance L'Heure Bleue, created by Jacques Guerlain in 1912, was the result of a summer holiday enjoying the bluish dusk and looking over the Baie de Somme. The saltmarsh lamb in this part of France is legendary, so it's natural that it should feature as one of the restaurant's signature dishes. I very much enjoyed it with this gravy, which had a definite aroma of early summer hay. Interestingly, they cook the lamb very rare, which I loved, but I remarked at the time that no one back home would accept the meat so red – unless they were on holiday in France, when it would seem perfectly OK. However, I've given quite a wide cooking time and the shorter will be rather more than pink. You can buy clean hay from pet shops and garden centres.

LEG OF LAMB COOKED IN HAY
GIGOT D'AGNEAU CUIT AU FOIN

SERVES 6–8

2–3 tbsp vegetable oil
1 leg of lamb, about 2.2kg
2 tbsp dried nori flakes
2 large cloves garlic, sliced
Large rosemary sprig,
    leaves removed and
    roughly chopped
A few thyme sprigs,
    leaves removed and
    roughly chopped
Fresh hay
Salt and black pepper

Gravy
150ml red wine
500ml Beef stock
    (page 301)
1 tbsp Beurre manié
    (page 303)

Heat the oil in a large frying pan and brown the leg of lamb on all sides. Add the nori flakes, garlic, rosemary and thyme and season with salt and pepper. Turn the leg of lamb over to coat it in the seasoning. Remove the lamb, then deglaze the pan with a little water and reserve that for the gravy.

Preheat the oven to 200°C/Fan 180°C. Arrange half the hay in the base of a large casserole dish with a lid or in a roasting tin. Put the leg of lamb with all the seasoning on the hay and cover it with the rest of the hay. Put the lid on or, if using a tin, cover with 2 or 3 layers of foil, sealing it well.

Cook the meat in the oven for 60–90 minutes until it is done to your liking. Check the internal temperature with a probe – 45°C will be very rare, 55°C medium rare and 60°C medium. Remove the lamb from the hay, picking off as many of the loose strands as you can, and leave it to rest for 15 minutes.

While the lamb is resting, make the gravy. Pour the wine, stock and deglazing liquid into the casserole dish with the hay, bring to the boil and reduce by a third. Pass through a sieve and put it back in the rinsed pan. Bring it to the boil, then whisk in the beurre manié to thicken the gravy. Add any juices from the resting lamb, then taste the gravy and season with salt and pepper.

Serve the lamb with the gravy and carrots à la fermière (page 250) or with roasted root vegetables and spinach or kale.

The Auberge de Sainte Maure is rather a charming restaurant beside the Melda river, just outside the city of Troyes in Champagne. I wanted to go there because I had heard that all the staff members were under 30, and I have a theory that often the most interesting cooking these days is in restaurants run by the young. What I particularly liked about it was that though the cooking is predictably a bit cheffy, it's actually very tasty and not over-garnished with tweezerage! There was a youthful enthusiasm among the staff and a great geniality from Julien Drapier, the head chef. I really liked this sweetbread dish. Troyes is a city that's well worth visiting. Its medieval centre is something of a revelation but also it's the main city of southern Champagne, which produces sparkling wines that are remarkably different to those of the north. Most notably they tend to have a vintage, whereas the house champagnes of such companies as Möet, Veuve Clicquot, Bollinger and so on are blends of years. That night I was introduced to Drappier, considered one of the finest boutique champagne producers in the world. A bottle of this is a good way to begin acquiring an enthusiasm for the champagnes of this region.

LAMB SWEETBREADS WITH LEMON & TARRAGON SAUCE

RIS D'AGNEAU AU CITRON ET À L'ESTRAGON MEUNIÈRE

SERVES 4
as a starter

400g plump lamb
    sweetbreads
½ tsp hot pimentón
50g Clarified butter
    (page 303)
Zest and juice of
    ½ small lemon
Small handful tarragon
    leaves, chopped
20 small asparagus
    spears, trimmed
150g button mushrooms,
    quartered
2 tbsp unsalted butter
Pea shoots, to garnish
Salt and black pepper

Place the sweetbreads in a bowl and rinse them under cold water. Leave them to soak for 30 minutes. Drain, put them in a pan and cover with water. Add 2 teaspoons of salt, then bring to a simmer for 2 minutes. Drain and leave to cool. Carefully peel away the outer membranes and set aside.

Season the sweetbreads with a quarter of a teaspoon of salt, the pimentón and some black pepper. Melt a third of the clarified butter in a frying pan until hot, add the sweetbreads and fry on all sides until golden (a couple of minutes per side depending on thickness).

Add the lemon zest and the remaining clarified butter to the pan and spoon over the sweetbreads, then add the chopped tarragon and lemon juice. Transfer the sweetbreads to a warm plate. Melt a tablespoon of the unsalted butter in the pan, add the asparagus and cook until tender, then season. Keep them warm while you cook the mushrooms in the same way.

Put some asparagus spears on each plate and top with the sweetbreads. Season with salt and pepper. Serve some of the button mushrooms alongside and spoon over a little butter sauce. Garnish with a few pea shoots.

Ah, the vicissitudes of filming. I understood that while in Cassis we were to be filming Djamal Boukhenifra, an Algerian fisherman, making a fish couscous with such delights as langoustines, bream, rascasse and dentex. I thought we would find ourselves in a little beach hut somewhere in a calanque, the rocky inlets that distinguish the coastline from Cassis to Marseille. In the event, we arrived at a very smart house on the outskirts of town to be told by the charming Djamal that he had decided to cook a chorba instead. A chorba is a North African stew flavoured with ras-el-hanout, which is a mixture of whatever spices are popular in the particular area of Algeria or Tunisia that the dish comes from. Apparently, some days 'there just ain't no fish'. I recall being a little disappointed to put it mildly to be having a lamb dish instead of fish, but in the event it turned out exceptionally well. I added some harissa to mine for a bit of extra oomph.

DJAMAL'S LAMB CHORBA

SERVES 4–5

2 tbsp olive oil
675g lean, boneless lamb
   shoulder (or mix of leg
   and shoulder), cut into
   2.5cm cubes
1 large red onion, chopped
2 cloves garlic, chopped
2 tbsp tomato paste
1½ tbsp harissa paste
1 tbsp ras-el-hanout
½ tsp ground ginger
400g tin chickpeas,
   drained and rinsed
90g orzo pasta
Handful fresh coriander
   leaves, chopped
Salt and black pepper

Heat a tablespoon of the oil in a large pan. Add the diced lamb, a batch at a time, and brown it all over; don't overcrowd the pan. Add the red onion and garlic and cook for a few minutes until softened, then add the tomato paste and harissa. Put the browned lamb back in the pan.

Pour in 1.5 litres of water and bring to a simmer. Add the ras-el- hanout, ginger, 1½ teaspoons of salt and the chickpeas, then cover the pan and leave to simmer for 30–40 minutes. Remove the lid and simmer for a further 10 minutes.

Add the orzo pasta and half the chopped coriander and cook for another 10 minutes until the pasta is tender. Taste for seasoning and add salt and pepper if necessary. Serve garnished with the remaining coriander.

I love a rack of lamb and I'm reminded of the time in Sydney when my stepchildren, Zach and Olivia, were very small. It was the first roast I cooked for them, and then a single rack was enough for the four of us, as they'd only have one cutlet each. Not the same now! Even then, I would put some garlic and rosemary under the joint to give flavour to the gravy I made with chicken stock, butter and a little lemon juice. The star turn of this dish is the dauphinoise. If there is any left over, blend it with chicken or vegetable stock to make a delicious soup the next day.

RACK OF LAMB WITH POTATO & CELERIAC DAUPHINOISE

CARRÉ D'AGNEAU ET GRATIN DAUPHINOISE POMMES DE TERRE ET CÉLERI-RAVE

SERVES 4–6

2 racks of lamb
1 tsp Rick's peppermix
    (page 303)
2 rosemary sprigs
2 cloves garlic, sliced
2 tsp olive oil
400ml Chicken stock
    (page 301)
1 tsp lemon juice
1 tbsp Beurre manié
    (page 303)

Dauphinoise
25g butter, at room
    temperature, plus
    extra for greasing
1 onion, finely sliced
2 cloves garlic,
    finely sliced
500ml double cream
1 tsp Dijon mustard
400g celeriac
600g potatoes,
    such as Maris Pipers
Salt and black pepper

Start with the dauphinoise. Preheat the oven to 180°C/Fan 160°C. Butter a 30 x 20cm gratin dish. Melt the butter in a large pan, add the onion and garlic and cook over a medium heat until softened. Add the double cream and mustard to the pan, season with 1½ teaspoons of salt and plenty of black pepper, then simmer for 5 minutes. Take the pan off the heat.

Cut the celeriac and potatoes into thin slices. Mix them with the cream mixture in the pan, then pour into the gratin dish and flatten the top. Bake for 1¼–1½ hours until the potatoes and celeriac are completely tender to the point of a knife.

Preheat the oven to 220°C/Fan 200°C. Season the racks with the peppermix. Put the rosemary, garlic and oil into a small roasting tin and sit the racks of lamb on top. Roast the racks for 15–20 minutes, then remove from the oven, transfer to a warm plate and cover with foil. Leave to rest for 10 minutes.

Set the roasting tin on the hob, add the stock and lemon juice and heat until reduced by half. Whisk in the beurre manié while the stock is still bubbling. Taste and check for seasoning, then pass the gravy through a sieve. Cut the racks into cutlets and serve with the gravy, dauphinoise and some green vegetables.

I do like a stuffed vegetable and this dish has all the varieties that you associate with the South of France. Tomatoes, courgettes, peppers and aubergines are stuffed with a little minced meat, parsley, Parmesan and rice, with a few chopped green olives for bite.

STUFFED VEGETABLES PROVENÇAL

PETITS FARCIS PROVENÇEAUX

SERVES 4–6

3 courgettes
  (each about 100g)
2 small aubergines
  (about 200g)
2 small red or yellow peppers
6 good-sized tomatoes
4 tbsp olive oil
250g veal or beef mince
250g pork mince
1 onion, chopped
2 cloves garlic, chopped
120g cold cooked rice
2 eggs, beaten
6 green olives,
  pitted and chopped
50g Parmesan cheese,
  freshly grated
Small handful flatleaf
  parsley, chopped
A few fresh thyme
  sprigs, leaves stripped
  and chopped
35g white breadcrumbs
Salt and black pepper

Cut the courgettes and aubergines in half lengthways. Remove the flesh from the middle of each one, leaving a slender wall around the edges. Chop the flesh and set it aside with the vegetable halves.

Cut the peppers in half through the stalk, then remove and discard the seeds. Take the top third off the tomatoes and scoop out the seeds. Add the tomato tops and seeds to the chopped courgette and aubergine.

Heat 2 tablespoons of the oil in a frying pan and brown the meats. Add the chopped vegetables, onion and garlic and cook for 10–15 minutes until lightly browned and the excess liquid from the vegetables has evaporated. Add the cooked rice, eggs, olives, half the Parmesan and the parsley and thyme, then season with salt and plenty of pepper.

Preheat the oven to 200°C/Fan 180°C and arrange the vegetables halves in a roasting tin. Fill them with the meat mixture, then mix the remaining Parmesan with the breadcrumbs and sprinkle on top. Drizzle over the remaining olive oil. Add 100ml of water to the tin and bake for 45 minutes. Serve hot with any juices.

Onglet is known as skirt in Britain and is actually the cut that we use for our Cornish pasties. It's also known as hanger steak and butchers' steak, on account of it being a particularly well-flavoured and tender cut but not well known, so a cut the butcher would keep for his own family. I suppose because of its distinctly open texture and the fact that it has a tough membrane running down the centre, hanger steak is not as beautiful as a sirloin but it tastes very good. This is a classic way of cooking it, just grilled and served with a sauce made with shallots, thyme, beef stock and red wine. *Recipe photograph overleaf.*

HANGER STEAK WITH SHALLOTS
L'ONGLET À L'ÉCHALOTE

SERVES 4

60g unsalted butter
1 x 800g onglet/hanger steak
  (or 2 x 400g)
250g shallots, finely sliced
1 thyme sprig
1 bay leaf
125ml red wine
100ml Beef stock (page 301)
Watercress, to garnish
Salt and black pepper

Heat a large frying pan over a high heat. Add a teaspoon of the butter and allow it to start melting, then add the steak. Fry until the steak is cooked to your liking – see timings below. Use a meat probe in the thickest part of the centre of the steak to check. Transfer the steak to a warm plate and cover it with foil to keep it warm while it rests.

Melt half the remaining butter in the same pan and add the shallots, thyme and bay leaf. Cook over a low heat for 8–10 minutes until the shallots have softened. Add the red wine and stock, turn the heat up to high and continue to cook until the liquid is reduced by half. Season with salt and plenty of pepper and remove the herbs. Whisk in any meat juices from the resting steak together with the remaining butter to thicken the sauce and make it glossy.

Cut the rested steak into thick slices and serve on a bed of shallots and sauce, with a little more sauce spooned over the meat. Scatter the watercress around the plate and serve with pommes purée (page 239).

Timings for 2cm-thick steaks
Blue: 1 minute each side (47–49°C)
Rare: 1½ minutes each side (50°C)
Medium rare: 2 minutes each side (55°C)
Medium: 2¼ minutes each side (60°C)
Medium well done 2½–3 minutes each side (65°C)
Well done: 4 minutes each side (71°c)

This recipe doesn't actually come from France, though to all intents and purposes it's French – the garlic, the red wine, the orange peel. I had it in Puerto Vallarta in Mexico and enjoyed it so much I vowed to one day get it into a book on French cooking. It's important to get the right short ribs for this. They are the elongated section of the ribs on a forequarter of beef, often called the Jacob's Ladder, comprising nine or ten rib bones; the best ones come from the middle section.

BRAISED BEEF SHORT RIBS

CÔTE DE BOEUF EN DAUBE

SERVES 8–10

4 tbsp olive oil
8-10 beef short ribs
   on the bone
1 large onion,
   roughly chopped
2 carrots, roughly chopped
1 celery stick,
   roughly chopped
4 cloves garlic, bashed
   with the heel of a knife
1 bottle of red wine
400g tinned tomatoes
2 strips of thinly pared
   orange peel
2 bay leaves
3 thyme sprigs
1.5 litres Beef stock
   (page 301)
1 tsp salt
1 tsp sugar
1 tsp Rick's peppermix
   (page 303)

**Vegetable and
pancetta garnish**
200g baby carrots
5 shallots, cut in half
   through the root
unsalted butter
½ tsp sugar
½ tsp salt
1 tbsp olive oil
250g button mushrooms
150g unsmoked pancetta,
   cut into 1cm dice
Handful flatleaf
   parsley, chopped

Heat the oil in a large flameproof casserole dish and brown the ribs all over, then set them aside. Add the onion, carrots, celery and garlic and cook over a low to medium heat until softened.

Put the ribs back in the casserole dish and add the red wine, tomatoes, orange peel, herbs and beef stock. Season with the salt, sugar and peppermix. Bring to a simmer, cover with a well-fitting lid and cook until the beef is tender and comes away easily from the bone – about 1½ hours. Transfer the ribs to a plate and cover them with foil while you finish the sauce.

Strain the liquid through a sieve into a bowl, pushing the vegetables down with the back of a ladle to extract as much flavour as possible. Discard the vegetables and herbs. Pour the liquid back into the casserole dish and boil hard to reduce by two-thirds to make a thickened and well-flavoured sauce.

For the vegetable and pancetta garnish, put the baby carrots and shallots in a shallow pan. Add 300ml of water and a tablespoon of butter, then season with the sugar and salt. Cover with a lid and bring to the boil, then simmer until the carrots and shallots are tender. Remove the lid and reduce the liquid to a sticky glaze.

In a separate small pan, fry the mushrooms and the pancetta together in a little butter for a couple of minutes. Add them to the carrots and shallots.

Put the ribs back in the sauce and warm them through for a minute or so, then add the carrots, shallots, mushrooms and pancetta. Serve topped with some chopped parsley.

Celeriac purée (page 251) or potato and celeriac dauphinoise (page 198) are good accompaniments.

This recipe comes from a little hotel we stayed at near Saint-Martin-Valmeroux in the Auvergne called Hostellerie de La Maronne. It's not the most original recipe, just fillet steak with a red wine and mushroom sauce, but it's designed, more than anything, to partner a heroic red wine. I can remember thinking at the time how grateful I was for something so simple, not the artistic creation of a starred chef. The sort of thing you might expect would be three little pieces of beef and a couple of tiny mushrooms in a shiny glazed 'jus', all contained in an enormous deep bowl, the sort of bowl in which your knife and fork slip down the sides so the handles get dunked in gravy. There might be a spear or two of chives and perhaps a pile of beef marrow and some tiny glazed onions, then something crisp and thin on top and finally a 'pillow' of foam. It might be beautiful but not enough to delight every gulp of wine as this dish did. I seem to remember the wine that night was a Cahors Clos de Gamot 2014 and the steak came with truffade, the local potato speciality – just potatoes and Cantal cheese cooked together. *Recipe photograph overleaf.*

FILLET STEAK WITH RED WINE & MUSHROOMS

FILET DE BOEUF AUX CHAMPIGNONS

SERVES 4

45g butter
100g chanterelle mushrooms,
    cleaned and quartered
    lengthways through
    the stalk
4 fillet steaks
    (each about 175g)
1 tbsp vegetable oil
1 shallot finely chopped
1 clove garlic, finely chopped
10g plain flour
75ml red wine
300ml Beef stock (page 301)
Salt and black pepper

Melt 15g of the butter in a large frying pan. Cook the mushrooms for a couple of minutes, then set them aside.

Brush the steaks on both sides with the oil and season well with salt and pepper. Heat a frying pan, add the steaks and cook them for 1–2 minutes per side for rare or up to 4 minutes per side for well done, depending on thickness (page 203). Use a meat probe in the thickest part of the centre of the steak to check. Place the steaks on a board or plate and cover them with foil to keep them warm.

Melt 20g of the butter in the pan. Add the shallot and garlic and fry until softened, then add the flour and cook for a moment longer. Pour in the red wine and reduce by half, then add the beef stock and bring to the boil to thicken. Add the mushrooms to warm through, then stir in the remaining butter. Check the seasoning.

Serve the steaks with the mushroom sauce spooned over and, ideally, some truffade (page 242).

Ariane Griffon and her son Paul run cookery classes from their 500-year-old farm in Puget sur Durance, Provence; they also make lovely olive oil. I was invited to have dinner with Ariane, Paul and a number of their friends, and the meal was preceded by an almost solo cookery lesson on real Provençal cuisine. They prepared anchoïade, fenouillade and stuffed tomatoes with persillade, everything built around a magnificent Rhône mariners' beef stew. The stew was delicious but requires two bottles of white Côtes du Rhône so I simply don't think anyone will cook it like that over here; it's too expensive and actually I need red wine in a Provençal stew. However, finishing a stew with anchoïade is so rewarding and I think accompanying it all with these very slow-cooked tomatoes is pretty special too. What I have stuck to is the long marinading and cooking time for the stew, and if you're interested, the wine they used was Maison Tardieu-Laurent Côtes du Rhône Blanc Guy Louis. I couldn't bring myself to empty a bottle or two of this wine into a stew. Sorry, Paul. Start preparing this dish a couple of days before you want to eat it.

RHÔNE MARINERS' STEW WITH ANCHOÏADE

SERVES 6

1kg onions, sliced
2kg chuck steak,
    cut into 6-7cm chunks
4-5 fresh thyme or
    oregano sprigs
2 bay leaves
5 cloves garlic, 25g,
    chopped or sliced
100ml olive oil
Zest of 1 orange
750ml Côtes du Rhône
    red wine
750ml Beef stock (page 301)
200g bacon lardons
Salt and white pepper

Tomatoes Provençal
Large handful
    flatleaf parsley
5 cloves garlic
2 tbsp olive oil
6 large tomatoes
Salt and black pepper

**Anchoïade (also known
as Beurre d'Avignon)**
3 cloves garlic, finely
    chopped or grated
3 salted anchovies
100g butter, softened
1 tbsp Dijon mustard

Mix the onions, meat, herbs, garlic, oil, zest and wine in a bowl. Season with white pepper and leave to marinate for 24 hours.

The next day, preheat the oven to 150°C/Fan 130°C. Pour everything into a flameproof casserole dish, bring to a simmer on the hob, then transfer the dish to the oven for 4 hours. Remove from the oven, leave to cool and then refrigerate.

The following day, preheat the oven to 150°C/Fan 130°C. Add the stock and lardons to the stew and bring it to a simmer on the hob as before. Put the dish in the oven and cook for a further 2 hours.

The tomatoes can be cooked at the same time. Chop the parsley with the garlic very finely, then mix with the oil and season with salt and pepper. Cut the top third off the top of each tomato (reserve the tops for a sauce or stock) and spoon over the parsley mixture. Place the tomatoes in a baking dish and cook for 1½ hours.

For the anchoïade, put the garlic in a pestle and mortar and pound it to a paste, or use a food processor. Add the anchovies and pound again to combine. Add half the soft butter and mix again, then add the remaining butter and continue to blend. Add the mustard and mix well.

Serve the stew with the tomatoes, pommes purée (page 239) and a bowl of anchoïade so everyone can help themselves.

In 1970 I went with a group of friends for a long weekend in Paris. We stayed at the Grand Hôtel de L'Univers, quite near the Boulevard St Germain, and virtually next door was a restaurant selling steak frites with red wine by the carafe – probably Beaujolais or Cabernet Franc from the Loire. They also sold Pinot Blanc from Alsace over the bar in tiny thick glasses with long green stems. It's not an exaggeration to say that the meal changed my life. Were they the best steak frites I have ever tasted? Being the first it's hard to tell, but ever since I have been trying to track down their equal. Finally, in Sainte-Christophe-en-Brionnais I found what I was looking for at a place called Restaurant du Midi in the high street. The steak was a large thin sirloin which was, I thought, unusual because I had been led to believe that rump was always used for steak frites. It was accompanied by the crispiest thin chips imaginable and, almost as important, soft lettuce, which used to be the only kind you could get before iceberg swept the board. Don't try to cook more than two steaks in a pan or they will stew and not fry and brown. *Recipe photograph overleaf.*

STEAK FRITES

SERVES 2

2 x 250g rump or sirloin
    steaks, well marbled
    with fat
Good pinch of salt
¼ tsp Rick's peppermix
    (page 303)
2 tsp rapeseed oil
10g butter

Frites
1 litre sunflower oil
500g Maris Piper
    potatoes, cut into
    4–5mm thick sticks
Salt

Green salad
½ soft round lettuce
2 tbsp sunflower oil
1 tsp white wine vinegar
Big pinch salt
Small pinch sugar

Start with the frites. Heat the oil in a deep pan to 125°C. Working in batches, cook the frites for about 3 minutes in the oil until they are limp but still pale. Drain each batch well on kitchen paper.

Season the steaks well on both sides with salt and peppermix. Brush a ridged griddle pan with oil and place it over a high heat. When the pan is hot, lay the steaks on the pan and cook them for 1–2 minutes per side for rare or up to 4 minutes per side for well done, depending on the thickness (page 203). Use a meat probe in the thickest part of the centre of the steak to check. When the steaks are done, add the butter to the pan and turn the steaks over to coat. Transfer the steaks to a plate, cover with foil and leave to rest for 5 minutes at room temperature.

While the steaks are resting, finish the frites. Heat the oil to 175°C and cook the frites, in batches, until golden and crisp (about 2 minutes). Drain them on kitchen paper and season well with salt. Whisk the ingredients for the dressing together and serve the steak with the frites and the salad.

Like boulangère potatoes, this dish would traditionally have been brought into the bakers for cooking in the still-hot oven after all the bread had been baked. It's one of those satisfying stews found all over Europe – some more lauded than others. In my *Food Heroes* series I travelled throughout the United Kingdom and Ireland looking for great producers and also great dishes, and in Merthyr Tydfil I became incredibly enthusiastic about a Welsh stew known as cawl. It's made of lamb or beef with leeks and cabbage. I did a bit of a vox pop in the restaurant where I ate it and predictably all the young said they didn't really like it; they preferred hamburgers. Baeckeoffe is an Alsatian speciality and fortunately seems to have remained a meaningful part of the culture, I suspect for two main reasons. One is the wonderfully decorative deep baking pot it's served in and the other is that Alsatian Sylvaner or Riesling wine must be used to make it. After long slow cooking, the wine gives the stew a delightful but restrained acidity that needs to be balanced with plenty of seasoning, hence the two teaspoons of salt.

ALSATIAN BEEF, LAMB & PORK STEW WITH POTATOES

BAECKEHOFFE

SERVES 8–10

750g boneless pork belly,
    cut into 4cm cubes
750g boneless lamb shoulder,
    cut into 4cm cubes
750g chuck steak,
    cut into 4cm cubes
2 onions, sliced
250g carrots, sliced
2 leeks, cut in half
    lengthways, washed
    and sliced
500ml Sylvaner or
    Riesling white wine
2kg potatoes, sliced into
    5mm thick rounds
100g unsmoked bacon,
    cut into 1cm pieces
250ml Beef stock (page 301)
Handful flatleaf parsley,
    roughly chopped,
    to garnish
Salt and black pepper

Place the meats, onions, carrots and leeks in a large, non-metallic bowl and pour over the wine. Cover and leave to marinate in the fridge overnight.

Preheat the oven to 190°C/Fan 170°C. You need a large casserole dish that has a lid. Arrange a quarter of the sliced potatoes in the base of the casserole dish. Drain the meats and vegetables in a colander over a bowl and reserve the juices. Scatter some of the vegetables over the potatoes, then add some bacon pieces and chunks of meat. Season with salt and pepper, then add another layer of potato and more vegetable, bacon, meat and seasoning. This does need plenty of salt – about 2 teaspoons in all. Repeat and finish with a final layer of potato, then pour over the reserved marinade juices and the beef stock. Cover the casserole dish with a tight-fitting lid and put it in the oven.

Bake for about 3 hours until the meat is tender. Garnish with chopped parsley and serve hot, straight from the oven.

Just as sometimes I feel that I visit too many markets in my films, I think I might also go to too many weird road stops off the beaten track, places that specialise in feeding truckers and tourists and that have a ramshackle shop overflowing with local produce. I was very much looking forward to having a plate of boles, Catalan meatballs, at a roadside shop-and-stop between Prades and Ille-sur-Têt. I expected sun-bleached plastic tables and chairs outside, the sort of place that people who follow my journeys might find disappointing when they see how scruffy it is. When I went there everything was as I had imagined, except they had stopped cooking for the season and there were no boles. This recipe came from a stall in Prades market where they were cooking boles in a huge paella pan and fabulous they were – beef and pork meatballs flavoured with cinnamon and piment d'Espelette in an exquisite tomato sauce with green olives, haricots and bacon, I thought there might be too much meat in the dish, but not at all.

BEEF & PORK MEATBALLS IN A TOMATO & 'PIMENT' SAUCE
BOLES DE PICOLAT

SERVES 4–6

400g minced beef
400g minced pork
1 egg
3 cloves garlic, finely
  chopped or grated
Small handful flatleaf
  parsley, chopped
½ tsp ground cinnamon
1 tsp piment d'Espelette
  (page 306) or pimentón
Plain flour
3 tbsp olive oil
Salt and black pepper

Sauce
1 tbsp olive oil
1 onion, finely chopped
100g unsmoked lardons
  or cubes of cooked ham
1 tsp piment d'Espelette
  (page 306) or pimentón
½ tsp ground cinnamon
6 tomatoes, hard cores
  removed, chopped
1 tbsp tomato paste
150g pitted green
  olives, drained
400g tin haricot
  beans, drained

In a large bowl, mix the meat, egg, garlic, parsley, cinnamon, piment d'Espelette and 2 tablespoons of flour. Season with salt and pepper and blend well. Using your hands, shape the mixture into golfball-sized balls, adding another tablespoon of flour if the mixture feels too wet to form into balls. Roll the balls in flour to lightly cover. Heat the oil in a large, preferably shallow, flameproof casserole dish, and brown the meatballs all over. Set them aside.

For the sauce, heat the tablespoon of olive oil in the same casserole dish and fry the onion and the lardons or ham until the onions are softened. Add the piment d'Espelette and cinnamon and cook for a minute, then add the chopped tomatoes, tomato paste and 250ml of water. Season with salt and pepper and bring to the boil. Turn the heat down, cover the pan and simmer for 15 minutes. Add the olives, haricot beans and browned meatballs to the sauce, together with any juices they have released.

Cover the pan and cook over a low heat for 30 minutes, then remove the lid and simmer for 10–15 minutes. Check a couple of times during cooking and add a little more water if the sauce looks as if it is getting too thick. Serve as a tapas or as a lunch or supper dish with pilaf rice (page 303).

Sas and I spend four days every year at La Colombe d'Or in Saint-Paul-de-Vence, near Nice. One of the reasons is because we can't believe how many marvellous paintings and sculptures are just nonchalantly placed in bedrooms, on stair landings, in the gents' loo, on the roof and by the pool, not to mention in the restaurant. This is one of my favourite dishes from La Colombe d'Or. I haven't asked them for the recipe but just written my own in the spirit of the dish. It's very much an à la minute treatment, relying not on a well-reduced tomato sauce but rather one briefly cooked and using the best possible tomatoes and oil, garlic and parsley. For me, it's important to make sure the kidneys are still pink in the centre, hence the short cooking time. Veal kidneys are not as easy to get hold of as lamb or pork, but they do have an exquisite delicacy of flavour and they're worth the extra money.

ROGNONS À LA PROVENÇAL

SERVES 4
as a starter or
2 as a main course

400g veal kidneys
2 tbsp olive oil
3 cloves garlic,
 finely chopped
4 ripe tomatoes, peeled,
 seeded and chopped
Small handful flatleaf
 parsley, chopped
Salt and black pepper

Remove any fat and the white core from each kidney. Cut the kidneys into 2cm cubes, trying to stick to the lobe pattern.

Heat a tablespoon of the oil in each of 2 non-stick frying pans. In one pan, gently fry the garlic, add the tomatoes and cook them for a few minutes until thick and pulpy. Season with half a teaspoon of salt and plenty of black pepper.

In the second pan, fry the kidneys for 2 minutes, then tip them into the tomato sauce and continue to cook them over a medium heat for a further minute. Stir through most of the chopped parsley and then serve immediately sprinkled with the remaining parsley. Good with fresh pasta, mashed potatoes or just with some crusty bread if served as a starter.

This is one of those dishes that fills me with happy and eager anticipation when I see it on the menu in a restaurant. I find that recipes like this one, hanger steak (page 203), steak frites (page 211) and chicken fricassée (page 150) are a great way of testing the skills of a kitchen. I like to finish the sauce with a little crème fraiche.

RABBIT STEW WITH DIJON MUSTARD

LAPIN À LA MOUTARDE DE DIJON

SERVES 4-6

2 young farmed rabbits, about 700g each, both jointed into 6 pieces
3 tbsp Dijon mustard
50g duck fat or Clarified butter (page 303)
200ml dry white wine
2 small or 1 large onion (200g), chopped
2 cloves garlic, finely chopped
100g smoked lardons or diced pancetta
1 heaped tbsp plain flour
500ml Chicken stock (page 301)
6-7 tarragon sprigs, leaves stripped from the stalks and chopped
60g full-fat crème fraiche
Salt and black pepper

Spread the rabbit joints with 2 tablespoons of the Dijon mustard. Cover them and refrigerate for at least 4 hours.

Heat half the duck fat or clarified butter in a flameproof casserole dish. Brown the rabbit pieces all over, then transfer them to a bowl. Deglaze the pan with the wine and add this to the rabbit.

Preheat the oven to 160°C/Fan 140°C. Heat the remaining fat in the pan and fry the onion, garlic and lardons or pancetta. When they have browned and softened a little, add the flour and cook for a minute or so. Then gradually add the chicken stock, stirring well after each addition to make sure there are no lumps.

Put the rabbit joints back in the casserole dish, cover and bring to a simmer. Put the dish in the oven and cook for 1¼ hours, until the rabbit is tender. (If using wild rabbit it will take longer than farmed.)

Remove the rabbit from the pan and keep it warm. Place the casserole dish on the hob and stir in the tarragon, crème fraiche and remaining mustard. Put the rabbit back in the dish and season with salt and pepper to taste. Serve with pilaf rice (page 303).

LÉGUMES

Glancing through the vegetable recipes in this chapter I'm struck by two things. First, it's quite clear to me now where all the good produce from the markets goes: to people's homes to make dishes like these, which you won't find in many restaurants. Second, that it's in vegetable dishes that French cooking seems so spot-on.

I particularly refer to a dish I ate in the Dordogne made by Christine Elias, who owns a walnut oil press near Périgueux. It was a simple haricot bean stew, made with lard, garlic, onions, tomatoes, haricot beans and parsley and finished with walnut oil, but most importantly she added a confit of pig's skin called couenne de porc – the bean recipe is on page 231. I don't know if something so obvious could be considered a tip, but if you're interested in writing recipes or creating dishes, do it when you're very hungry. Your understanding of the subtleties of good cooking, the aromas and flavours, is much accentuated. You would have thought that the idea of adding fatty pig skin to a perfectly decent vegetable dish would be quite unpleasant, but not to me that morning after an inspiring visit to the walnut mill. I was very hungry and filled with thoughts of the richness of the produce of Aquitaine, not just walnuts, black truffles and foie gras but also cheeses, particularly the Rocamadour that I'd tried in the Périgueux market early that morning, and a number of 'everything but the squeal' parts of the pig. Maybe it's just me looking for nuances in cooking but it did seem that the taste of that soft, salty pork skin in the bean stew was like a view into a different world of local flavour, where food, country and the people make the cuisine du terroir.

If I were going to describe what I mean by Secret France it's moments like these. Sadly, perhaps, we live in a world where you can get most things everywhere. The time I like to look back to in France was when where you couldn't even get Bonne Maman jam anywhere but there. Countries were much more different from each other then, but I'm still looking to find those differences. 'Vive la différence' say the French about the sexes. I say the same about cuisines, and yet I seem to spend my time trying to unearth those differences and perhaps thereby helping to make them not secret at all.

Ah well. I was filmed in Jura last year in a little bar lost in time and I just said to the camera, 'Go and find it yourself!'

This dish is very much of the 1980s/90s and the sort of thing I'd forgotten about until I had it for lunch at Les Maisons de Concasty in the Auvergne. The Auberge is in the beautiful Cantal countryside and has some very comfortable rooms, plus Martine's cooking. She made this dish as an accompaniment to a loin of lamb, but being a man of simple tastes, I still prefer fairly plain vegetables with perfectly cooked pink lamb, as this was. I thought the charlottine so good, though, and it has such nostalgic memories for me, but I prefer to serve it on a disc of puff pastry with a simple cream sauce enlivened with some Parmesan. If you like, you could use asparagus instead of courgettes.

'CHARLOTTINE' OF COURGETTES WITH CREAM & PARMESAN

SERVES 6

350g courgettes, chopped
1 tsp fine table salt
150–200g puff pastry
3 eggs, plus 3 extra egg yolks
250ml double cream
Small handful chives, chopped
Butter, for greasing
Salt and black pepper

Cream sauce
100ml double cream
2 tbsp freshly grated Parmesan cheese
A few chives, chopped

Put the courgettes in a colander over a bowl and sprinkle them with the salt. Leave for 30 minutes.

Preheat the oven to 210°C/Fan 190°C. Roll out the pastry if necessary and cut 6 discs of puff pastry, each 9–10cm in diameter. Place these on a baking sheet and bake for 8–10 minutes until risen, crisp and golden. Set aside. Turn the oven down to 160°C/Fan 140°C.

Put the courgettes in a food processor and add the eggs, extra yolks, cream and chives, then season with salt and pepper. Blitz for 1–2 minutes to make a thick custard.

Butter 6 individual pudding moulds or ramekins 8–9cm in diameter. Put the moulds in a deep roasting tin. Pour the mixture into the moulds, then add boiling water to the tin to reach halfway up the sides of the moulds. Bake in the oven for 18–20 minutes, until the custards are just set with a little wobble, but not rubbery.

For the sauce, pour the cream into a pan and warm over a low heat. Stir in the grated Parmesan and season with black pepper.

Put a pastry disc on each plate. Run the tip of a knife round each charlottine and turn out on to the pastry. Drizzle with sauce, sprinkle with chives and serve at once. If you have trouble turning the charlottines out, dip the moulds or ramekins in hot water briefly, then turn them out.

Confiting such vegetables as tomatoes and aubergines in the autumn in Provence is not only an obvious way of preserving them but also serves to intensify the flavour of both, particularly when they're accompanied by such things as thyme, olive oil and garlic. I'm of a time when throwing away food was almost a sin – and it is again now – so if I'm going away on a trip I always spend a couple of hours pickling, reducing and making confit or soups. If I run out of time I freeze the ingredients to deal with when I get back. For me, simple confits of aubergines and tomatoes are what makes Mediterranean cooking so appealing. And then you can come up with a tart like the one on page 228 in no time.

CONFIT AUBERGINES

600g (about 2) aubergines,
   sliced into rounds
1 tbsp fine salt
300ml olive oil
5 cloves garlic, chopped
A few fresh thyme sprigs
1–2 small dried chillies or a
   large pinch of chilli flakes
4 salted anchovy fillets,
   chopped (optional)

Put the aubergine slices in a colander and sprinkle them with salt, then turn them over and sprinkle the other side. Set the colander over a bowl and leave for 30 minutes. Rinse the slices and dry them with kitchen paper. Discard any juices. Preheat the oven to 110°C/Fan 90°C.

Pour the oil into a small roasting tin and add the garlic, thyme, chillies and anchovies, if using. Warm the oil on the hob, then submerge the aubergines slices in the oil. Put the tin in the oven and cook for about 2 hours.

Pack the aubergine slices into sterilised jars and top up with the flavoured oil. Screw on the lids and leave to cool, then store in the fridge. Allow to come up to room temperature before using to liquefy the oil.

CONFIT TOMATOES

1kg tomatoes, cut in half
2 cloves garlic, bashed
   but left whole
A few fresh thyme sprigs
200ml olive oil
1 tbsp balsamic vinegar
Salt and black pepper

Preheat the oven to 110°C/Fan 90°C. Arrange the tomatoes, cut-side up, in a roasting tin just big enough to hold them in one layer and season with salt and pepper. Nestle the garlic cloves and thyme sprigs among the tomatoes, then pour over the oil and balsamic vinegar.

Put the tomatoes in the oven and cook them for 2–2½ hours. Pack into sterilised jars with the juices and oil and allow to cool, then store in the fridge. Allow to come up to room temperature before using to liquefy the oil.

I find that I'm increasing the number of vegetarian dishes in my books more and more. This is mainly because people keep asking me for them, but also I think most of us eat too much meat, and dishes like this are simply superb in their own right. I have specified an all-butter puff pastry here, but if you want to make this a lovely vegan dish, use a margarine-based pastry. There's a recipe for green pistou, a French version of pesto, on page 302, and a teaspoonful with a slice of this tart is fabulous.

CONFIT TOMATO & AUBERGINE TARTE TATIN

SERVES 2–3
as a main course with salad

1 garlic clove, cut in half
½ quantity Confit tomatoes (page 225), well drained of oil
½ quantity Confit aubergines (page 225) well drained of oil, omitting the anchovies
½ tsp herbes de Provence
250g all-butter puff pastry
Leaves from a few thyme sprigs
1–2 tbsp Green pistou (page 302 – optional)
Salt and black pepper

Preheat the oven to 200°C/Fan 180°C. You need a 20cm fixed-base cake tin or an ovenproof frying pan. Rub the inside of the tin or pan with the cut garlic clove, then arrange the tomatoes, cut-side down, over the base. Next arrange a layer of about 8 slices of aubergine over the tomatoes. Sprinkle with the herbes de Provence and season with salt and pepper.

Roll out the puff pastry into a disc a little larger than the tin or pan to allow for shrinkage and place it over the aubergines. Bake the tart for 25–30 minutes, until the pastry has risen and is golden and crisp.

Remove the tart and allow it to cool a little. Carefully cover the tin or pan with a plate and invert to turn the tart out. You may need to rearrange a few of the vegetables with a palette knife if dislodged and blot up any oil spills on the plate.

Sprinkle with the thyme leaves and serve warm or at room temperature with a little pistou on the side, if using, and a green salad.

For years, whenever I got a haricots verts salad and admired the way each bean was neatly halved lengthways, I assumed there was some machine or knife technique to do it. Then a friend told me that you just boil the beans and separate them by hand, and of course that's what they do to produce such fine green lengths. This vegetable accompaniment is made more interesting by the chapelure – fried breadcrumbs.

SPLIT GREEN BEANS WITH GARLIC & FRIED BREADCRUMBS

HARICOTS VERTS À L'AIL ET CHAPELURE

SERVES 4

500g fine green beans
    (haricots verts), trimmed
25g butter
2 tbsp extra virgin olive oil
4 cloves garlic, grated
    or finely chopped
2 tbsp panko breadcrumbs
Small handful flatleaf
    parsley, chopped
Salt and black pepper

Bring a pan of water to the boil, add half a teaspoon of salt and boil the beans for 4 minutes. Refresh in cold water, then drain and pull them apart lengthways.

Heat the butter and oil in a non-stick frying pan and add the garlic and breadcrumbs. Fry over a medium heat for a couple of minutes until golden, then add the beans and chopped parsley. Season with salt and pepper and stir for a minute or so to heat through. Serve immediately.

This recipe contains a must-have ingredient that may deter some from making it – confit pork skin (couenne de porc). You can buy it in tins in the Dordogne, where this recipe comes from. I am a bit of a fan of some of the less appealing parts of French cuisine, such as andouillettes, the aromatic tripe sausages, or violets, the deeply bitter, creamy yellow interior of a leathery Mediterranean sea creature that clings to rocks. All these add to my interest in unusual ingredients that make local cooking unique. It's often difficult to replicate these flavours elsewhere but not a big problem here, as I've included a recipe for confit pork skin on page 303. The other important ingredient is the walnut oil, which finishes the dish. The recipe comes from Christine Elias, at Le Moulin de la Veyssière near Neuvic in Périgord, who owns what is perhaps the best of all walnut oil presses. She cooked this for me and finished it by drizzling some of her wonderful oil over the beans.

HARICOT BEANS WITH CONFIT PORK SKIN

HARICOTS À LA PÉRIGOURDINE

SERVES 4

500g dried haricot beans
2 onions, chopped
4 large ripe tomatoes, skinned and chopped
60g Confit pork skin (page 303), chopped into 5mm dice
2 tbsp lard, at room temperature
4 cloves garlic, chopped
Handful flatleaf parsley, chopped
3 tbsp walnut oil
Salt and black pepper

Soak the beans in cold water overnight, then drain and rinse them. Put them in a large pan and cover with about 1.5 litres of fresh cold water – exactly how much will depend on the size of your pan, but the beans should be just covered by 2cm of water.

Add the chopped onions and tomatoes and season with 2 teaspoons of salt and plenty of pepper. Bring to the boil, then turn down the heat to a gentle simmer and cook for 1½ hours. By this time the beans should be fairly tender and the consistency of the dish should be soupy. Add a little water if it looks too dry.

Stir in the pieces of pork skin. In a bowl, mash the lard with a wooden spoon and stir in the garlic and parsley to make a paste. Stir this into the beans, then check the seasoning and add more salt and pepper if necessary. Cook the beans over a low heat for a further 30 minutes, then serve drizzled with walnut oil. This makes a good lunch with some crusty bread and salad.

This is designed to accompany the deep-fried pork chops on page 183. Chef Harry Lester served them to us one sunny Sunday morning at a table outside his restaurant in Clermont-Ferrand. It seemed to me at the time that he had well understood the French way with good produce and simplicity.

BRAISED PEAS WITH LARDONS

PETITS POIS AUX LARDONS

SERVES 4
as a side dish

30g butter
1 medium onion,
    finely chopped
100g smoked bacon
    lardons
2 tsp plain flour
200ml Chicken or
    Vegetable stock
    (page 301)
450g frozen or
    freshly shelled peas,
    about 1.25kg of pods
    to yield 450–500g
¼ tsp sugar
Salt and black pepper

Melt the butter in a pan and cook the onion and lardons for about 5 minutes over a low heat until the onions have started to soften. Stir in the flour and cook for a minute or two, then add the stock and bring to the boil.

Turn down the heat, add the fresh or frozen peas. Cover with a lid and cook for 15–20 minutes. Check during the cooking time and add a little more water if necessary; the peas should be just submerged in the liquid while cooking. The finished dish should have a slightly soupy consistency.

Season with the sugar, salt and plenty of pepper.

Is there anything more gorgeous than lots of onions cooked with butter for up to an hour? In this recipe, they're simply combined in a shortcrust pastry case with egg yolks and cream and then baked. This dish comes from Alsace and is the sort of tart the French do so well. Go easy with the nutmeg. Just a soupçon, or maybe une ombre, is enough, but it does make a difference. *Recipe photograph overleaf.*

ONION TART FROM ALSACE

TARTE À L'OIGNON ALSACIENNE

SERVES 4–6

Pastry
225g plain flour,
    plus extra for rolling
½ tsp salt
130g cold unsalted
    butter, cubed
1 egg yolk
1–2 tbsp ice-cold water

Filling
60g butter
800g onions, finely sliced
200ml double cream
4 egg yolks, beaten
A rasp or 2 of freshly
    grated nutmeg
Salt and black pepper

For the pastry, put the flour, salt and butter in a food processor and pulse until you have a mixture resembling breadcrumbs. Transfer it to a bowl, add the egg yolk and just enough of the water to bring the dough together; too much water makes tough pastry.

Turn the dough out on to a lightly floured board. Roll it out to a circle about 26cm in diameter and use it to line a 23cm loose-bottomed flan tin. Cover and refrigerate for 30–40 minutes.

While the pastry is chilling, make the tart filling. Melt the butter in a large pan and add the onions, stirring to coat them in butter. Cover the pan with a lid and cook the onions over a low heat for 30–45 minutes until they are meltingly soft and sweet. Check the onions occasionally and give them a stir. Take the pan off the heat, stir in the double cream and the egg yolks, then season with salt, pepper and nutmeg. Set aside. Preheat the oven to 200°C/Fan 180°C.

Line the pastry case with greaseproof paper and baking beans, then bake for about 10 minutes. Remove the beans and paper and put the pastry back in to the oven for 3–4 minutes to dry out the base a little. Turn the oven down to 170°C/Fan 150°C.

Pour the onion mixture into the pastry case and bake for 20–25 minutes or until just set. Serve warm or at room temperature with a green salad.

This is the French version of rosti potatoes – the word paillasson means mat. So often I find that the title of a dish sounds so much better in French.

FRENCH POTATO CAKE

POMMES PAILLASSON

SERVES 4

800g Maris Piper potatoes
4 tbsp unsalted butter, melted
2 tbsp olive oil
Salt and black pepper

Peel the potatoes and cut them into fine julienne strips, either in a food processor or on a mandoline. Put them in a colander over a bowl, season with a teaspoon of salt and let them sit for a few minutes to release some of their liquid.

Heat 2 tablespoons of the butter and a tablespoon of oil in a 25cm non-stick frying pan over a medium heat. Pile the potatoes on to a clean tea towel and squeeze out as much water as possible and then put them in the pan. Use the back of a wooden spoon to flatten them into a cake.

Cook over a medium heat for about 15 minutes until crispy and brown, then remove the pan from the heat and leave to cool a little. Place a plate over the pan, then turn the pan over to flip the potato cake on to the plate. Add the rest of the butter and oil to the pan, then slide the cake back in, uncooked side down. Cook for another 10 minutes until the cake is crispy underneath and the potatoes have cooked through.

Slide the cake on to a board and blot any excess grease with kitchen paper. Cut into wedges, season with salt and pepper, and serve immediately.

For me, the success of perfect pommes purée lies in adding plenty of butter and milk or olive oil, but not too much. So often with a rich red wine stew like a daube, the accompanying potato can be too rich. The object is to achieve the perfect balance.

POMMES PURÉE

SERVES 4

1kg floury potatoes,
    cut into chunks
300ml whole milk
50g butter, at room
    temperature
Salt and black pepper

Put the potatoes in a pan of salted water, bring to the boil and simmer for 20 minutes. Drain the potatoes in a colander and allow them to steam and air dry.

Press the potatoes through a ricer or a Mouli (a regular masher doesn't give a smooth enough result).

Tip the potatoes back into the pan, add the milk and butter, then beat over a low heat until light and smooth. Season with salt and pepper to taste.

For the olive oil version, cook and mash as above, then beat in 90-100ml olive oil and 50-100ml of milk. Beat over a low heat until light and smooth, then season to taste.

This dish is probably the most famous Auvergne recipe and is simply sliced potatoes, lard and young Cantal cheese cooked with a little garlic and pork fat. In the UK it's impossible to get the exact type of cheese, which is called Tomme de Cantal; it's made from skimmed milk when the cream has been used to make butter or richer cheeses, so it's low in fat and high in acidity. The best choice in the UK would be a very young Cheddar. It's normal in the Auvergne to cook the potatoes from raw, but I find it much more controllable to parboil them first.

CRUSHED POTATOES WITH CHEESE

LA TRUFFADE

SERVES 4–6

6 baking potatoes,
about 1.4kg
25g lard
50g pork back fat or
pancetta, finely diced
2 large garlic cloves,
finely chopped
400g Cantal or young
Cheddar cheese, grated
Salt and black pepper

Peel the potatoes and slice them into 5mm rounds. Put them in a pan of plenty of salted water, bring to the boil and cook for 5–6 minutes, then drain.

Melt the lard in a large, heavy-based frying pan or a shallow flameproof casserole dish. Add the back fat or pancetta and cook to render down the fat. Continue until the fat turns brown, then add the garlic, then the potatoes, pushing them down to break them up a bit. Add the cheese on top of the potatoes and season with salt and pepper.

Keep the pan over a low heat while the potatoes cook and the cheese begins to melt, then start to turn the potatoes and cheese, trying not to break them up too much. Continue to cook and turn every few minutes for about 15 minutes.

Cut the truffade into wedges or serve in large spoonfuls. The cheese will be stringy and the crust a deep golden brown.

When making my *Long Weekends* series about visiting various European cities, we quite often filmed aspects of life on the road, like trundling luggage along cobbled streets or dealing with the perplexities of coffee and juice machines at hotel breakfasts. Another thing that I liked was finding some surprising dish on the menu and getting the chef to cook it for me in the hotel kitchen; this risotto was a case in point. Mélissa, the chef at the Golden Tulip Hotel in Troyes, turned out to have worked at a two-Michelin-star restaurant nearby and the vegetarian risotto that she cooked was really good. She used quinoa, which I find a bit tasteless, so I've taken her basic ingredients and used pearled spelt grains instead – you could also use pearl barley. I finish it with a little butter and Parmesan, but I've also made a version with nutritional yeast flakes, the vegan umami standby, which is very good too. *Recipe photograph overleaf.*

SPELT RISOTTO WITH SPRING VEGETABLES
RISOTTO DE PETIT ÉPEAUTRE AUX LÉGUMES

SERVES 3–4

2 tbsp olive oil
1 large onion, chopped
2 cloves garlic, chopped
300g pearled spelt
100ml dry white wine
1 litre Vegetable stock
    (page 301)
45g butter
40g Parmesan cheese,
    finely grated
8 baby carrots, halved
    lengthways, keeping
    green tops if possible
150g baby turnips,
    finely sliced
¼ tsp sugar
100g fine green beans,
    trimmed and cut into
    2cm lengths
100g broad beans, double
    podded, fresh or frozen
100g peas, fresh or frozen
1 tbsp fresh chopped fines
    herbes (page 306)
Salt and black pepper

Heat the oil in a pan, add the onion and garlic and cook until soft. Add the spelt, stir to coat it with the oil, then add the white wine and stir until it's been absorbed. Add the hot vegetable stock a ladleful at a time, stirring after each addition, and cook until all is absorbed and the spelt grain is tender. This will take 25–30 minutes. Stir in 30g of the butter and three-quarters of the Parmesan, then season with salt and plenty of pepper.

While the risotto is cooking, put the carrots and turnips in a saucepan, add 100ml of water, the remaining butter, quarter of a teaspoon of salt and the sugar. Cover with a lid and bring to the boil, then reduce the heat to a simmer and cook until the carrots and turnips are just tender. Remove the lid and cook until the vegetables are slightly caramelised and the water has evaporated. Set them aside in the pan.

Bring a pan of salted water to the boil and cook the fine green beans and the fresh broad beans and peas, if using. Cook for 4 minutes, drain well and add them to the pan of root vegetables. If using frozen broad beans and peas, just add them at this stage. Add a tablespoon of water and the herbs, put the pan back on the heat and continue to cook briefly, tossing the vegetables until they are glistening and evenly coated in the herbs. Fold the vegetables through the spelt risotto and check the seasoning. Sprinkle over the remaining Parmesan cheese and serve immediately.

If you'd like to make this recipe vegan, use 2 teaspoons of nutritional yeast instead of the Parmesan, and another 3 tablespoons of olive oil instead of the butter.

This recipe evolved over years of cooking in my restaurant in Padstow. As far as I remember, one of the many Frenchmen who passed through my kitchen introduced me to it, particularly the lovely word mélange. Somehow mixture doesn't quite add up to mélange – it's more subtle, like mijouter, to simmer, or moelleux, meaning soft. I insist that this contains lightly caramelised carrots – they can be frozen – but everything else is down to what you have. Sometimes I add broad beans, sometimes haricot, sometimes flageolet but always tarragon.

VEGETABLE MÉLANGE
WITH FRESH HERBS

SERVES 4

8 baby carrots, halved
    lengthways, keeping
    green tops if possible
6 baby turnips, finely sliced
20g butter
¼ tsp sugar
100g fine green beans,
    cut into 2cm lengths
100g peas, fresh or frozen
100g broad beans, double
    podded, frozen are fine
2 tbsp fresh herbs, chopped
    (tarragon, flatleaf parsley,
    chives and chervil)
Salt and black pepper

Put the carrots and turnips in a pan and add the butter, sugar and 100ml of water. Season with salt and bring to the boil, then reduce to a simmer and cover with a lid. Cook until the carrots and turnips are tender, then remove the lid and continue to cook until they are lightly caramelised. Remove the pan from the heat and set aside to keep warm.

Bring a pan of salted water to the boil and cook the fine beans, broad beans and fresh peas, if using. Cook for 4 minutes, drain well and add them to the pan of root vegetables. If using frozen peas, just add them at this stage. Add a tablespoon of water and the herbs and stir to coat the vegetables with the glistening herby juices. Season with salt and black pepper and serve immediately.

Bitter vegetables are not much used in our part of the world compared with say, in India or Greece, where they gather bitter leaves, boil them and serve them with olive oil and lemon juice. The exception is chicory and it almost seems to me that bitterness has the same satisfying effect as chillies with heat. I like to wrap each piece of chicory in a little bit of prosciutto to give it extra oomph, but you can make this without as a vegetarian dish. It would make either a lovely main course or a side dish. Incidentally, chicory is one of the most popular vegetables in Picardy. *Recipe photograph overleaf.*

CHICORY GRATIN
ENDIVE AU GRATIN

SERVES 4
as a side or 2 as a main

4 heads of pale yellow chicory (450–500g)
Thick slice of lemon
30g butter, plus extra for greasing the dish
30g plain flour
400ml whole milk
1 tbsp Dijon mustard
135g Comté or Gruyère cheese, grated
8 slices Parma ham or cooked ham (optional)
30g coarse sourdough breadcrumbs
Salt and black pepper

Rinse and trim the heads of chicory and cut them in half lengthways. Place them cut side down in a shallow pan, ideally just large enough to accommodate them all in one layer. Pour over enough water to cover and add a few pinches of salt and pepper and a thick slice of lemon. Bring the water to a simmer, then cover the pan with a lid and cook gently until the chicory is tender when prodded with a knife. This can take 10–20 minutes depending on the size.

Melt the butter in a pan, stir in the flour and cook over a medium heat for a couple of minutes. Gradually whisk in the milk until it is all incorporated and keep stirring while you bring the sauce to the boil. Continue to stir for a couple of minutes until thickened, then stir in the mustard and 75g of the grated cheese. Season the sauce with salt and pepper and set it aside. Preheat the oven to 180°C/Fan 160°C.

Drain the chicory halves really well. If using ham, wrap each chicory half in a piece of ham. Butter an oven dish, which will accommodate the chicory in a single layer, then arrange them cut-side down.

Pour over the cheese sauce, then mix the rest of the cheese with the breadcrumbs and sprinkle over the top. Season with freshly ground black pepper.

Bake in the preheated oven for 20–25 minutes until golden brown and bubbling. Serve with a green salad and crusty bread.

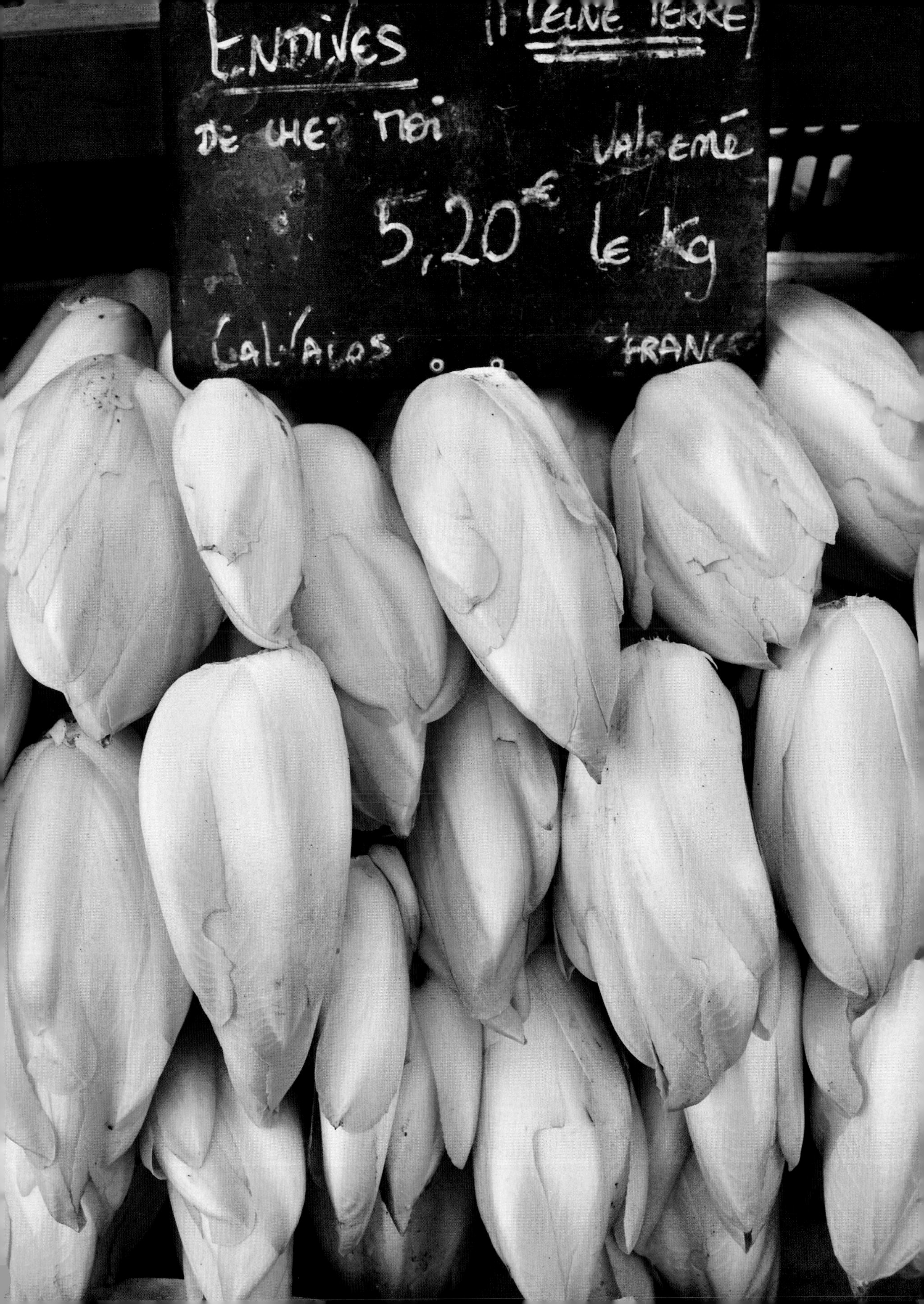
ENDIVES
(PLEINE TERRE)
DE CHEZ MOI
VALSEMÉ
5,20€ le kg
CALVADOS

I'm a bit of a pushover for buying art books in museums and galleries. This recipe comes from the *Monet Cook Book: Recipes from Giverny,* which I bought at the Musée de l'Orangerie in Paris, where eight of Monet's great water lily paintings are spectacularly displayed.

CARROTS À LA FERMIÈRE

SERVES 6
as a side

1kg large, fresh carrots, sliced into rounds
30g butter
30g flour
Small handful flatleaf parsley and tarragon, chopped
Juice of 1 lemon
2 tsp caster sugar
Salt and black pepper

Put the carrots in a pan of water and season with a teaspoon of salt. Cook the carrots for 12–15 minutes until tender but not soft, then drain and reserve the cooking water.

Melt the butter in a large frying pan and whisk in the flour. Gradually add about 250ml of the cooking liquid, whisking all the time to avoid lumps. Add the chopped herbs and plenty of black pepper, bring to the boil and boil for 2 minutes to thicken.

Add the lemon juice and sugar, then put the carrots back in the pan and cover loosely with a lid. Leave a small gap to allow some steam to escape. Add a little more of the cooking water, then simmer over a very low heat for about 30 minutes. Stir gently from time to time but take care not to break up the carrots. When cooked, they should be soft and coated in the glistening sauce.

This is a version of a great potato dish from the Auvergne, which is basically garlic mashed potatoes with cheese. It's usually cooked with one of the local Tome cheeses, notably Tome de Laguiole, which is made from skimmed milk so is reasonably low in fat. It's hard to get, though, so I often use Emmental.

ALIGOT

SERVES 4

1kg floury potatoes,
 cut into chunks
60g butter, cut into cubes
3 cloves garlic, finely
 chopped or grated
250g Emmental cheese,
 grated
100-150ml whole milk
Salt

Put the potatoes in a pan of salted water, bring to the boil and simmer for about 20 minutes until tender. Drain the potatoes, then mash roughly.

Add the butter, garlic, cheese and a teaspoon of salt to the pan of hot mash and, using an electric hand whisk, whisk in enough milk to get a light fluffy consistency. I usually add about 125ml.

Eat this on its own, maybe with a salad, or serve as a thoroughly OTT addition to a pork chop or steak.

At The Seafood Restaurant in Padstow I like to organise the sweets section of the menu into six categories. First, chocolate: things like mousses, pavés and soufflés. This is followed by anything to do with lots of cream, particularly set creams like creme brûlée, crème caramel and panna cotta. In the next section there are tarts: fruit tarts like tarte tatin, lemon or fig, and comforting ones like walnut. Next, I insist on a nursery pudding such as bread and butter, treacle or spotted dick. I always want there to be a light fruit-based sweet, perhaps just a take on strawberries or raspberries or something like an îles flottantes with rhubarb, and lastly there must be an elaborate 'haute cuisine' type of dish. I often leave this one to the pastry chef's dexterity and it might have twirls, balls, wafer-thin slices of dried fruit and neat lozenges of sorbet moulded in teaspoons, though I draw the line at smears, particularly chocolate ones. In this way, we try to cover the whole spectrum of what might tempt our customers; the last thing we want is to have them say, 'No thanks. I'll leave it'.

Big tempters here are lemon soufflé, simple fruit tarts and chocolate mousse, and in the nursery pudding section, sticky toffee or steamed treacle sponge. My cooking style is determinedly simple but I make an exception with desserts, mainly because I am particularly fond of elaborate French pâtisserie.

Two recipes in this chapter are exactly what I'm talking about. Including them was a bit of a leap of faith because they are complicated to make and I know everyone likes simple these days, but once in a while it's really rather good fun to make such things as the coffee, almond and hazelnut meringue known in French as dacquoise on page 266, or the raspberry vacherin semifreddo on page 274.

The other great tempters on sweet menus are ice creams. I often just go for plain vanilla, as it's a way of satisfying a craving but arguing to myself that I'm not really giving in to the extreme naughtiness of some calorie-packed stunner, but if such a dish as kougelhopf glacé (page 268) was on offer, I think I would be a bit of a pushover.

This chapter has been a great pleasure to write. Desserts are one area of cooking where I would say that the French still rule the roost.

The idea for these little tarts comes from the delightful southern town of Uzès. At dinner one night, I had a fig tart and was intrigued by the fact that it had this delicious moelleux texture in the centre. On leaving, I asked for the recipe and was told, sorry, they bought it in. Sadly, this happens so much in French restaurants – the cost of staff I'm afraid. What I took to be subtlety was probably simply that the tart had been cooked from frozen and was still slightly underdone in the centre. This is a proper version and quite delicious. I favour crème fraiche with these.

FIG & FRANGIPANE TARTS
TARTES FRANGIPANE AUX FIGUES

MAKES 6 X 10–12CM TARTLETS

Shortcrust pastry
170g plain flour, plus extra for rolling
100g cold unsalted butter, cubed
Pinch of salt
1 egg yolk
1–2 tbsp ice-cold water

Filling
100g butter, at room temperature
100g caster sugar
2 eggs, beaten
½ tsp almond extract
100g ground almonds
9 figs, quartered
1 tbsp flaked almonds

To serve
1 tsp icing sugar
6 tbsp crème fraiche

For the pastry, put the flour, butter and salt in a food processor and pulse until the mixture resembles breadcrumbs. Transfer to a bowl and add the egg yolk mixed with a tablespoon of cold water to make a smooth but not sticky dough. Add the extra water if required.

Put the dough on a floured work surface, roll it out and line 6 loose-bottomed 10–12cm tartlet tins. Chill for about 30 minutes. Preheat the oven to 200°C/Fan 180°C.

Line each tin with a circle of baking parchment or foil, add baking beans and bake blind for 10 minutes. Remove the beans and paper, then put the tins back in the oven for a further 5 minutes. Turn the oven down to 190°C/Fan 170°C.

While the pastry cases are cooking make the frangipane. Beat the butter and sugar together in a bowl until you have a smooth paste. Gradually whisk in the eggs and almond extract, then stir in the ground almonds and mix well. Divide the mixture between the pastry cases and arrange 6 fig wedges on top of each tart. Scatter with some of the flaked almonds and bake for 20–25 minutes until golden. Dust with a little icing sugar and serve warm or at room temperature with some crème fraiche.

These soufflés are very light and fluffy and can be made in advance up to the stage before the egg whites are whisked and added. Do have everything ready to serve, as the soufflés sink rapidly. The combination of the hot soufflé and cold sorbet is the sort of touch that transforms these into something memorable, particularly because of the colours. By the way, these can be made very successfully using gluten-free plain flour.

HOT LEMON SOUFFLÉS WITH RASPBERRY SORBET

SERVES 6

45g butter, plus 10g melted
   butter for greasing
70g caster sugar, plus extra
   for dusting the ramekins
30g plain flour
15g cornflour
225ml whole milk
Grated zest of 2
   unwaxed lemons
4 tbsp fresh lemon juice
4 eggs, separated
Icing sugar, to dust (optional)

To serve
Raspberry sorbet (page 274)

Preheat the oven to 200°C/Fan 180°C. Put a heavy baking tray into the oven to heat up.

Brush the insides of the ramekins with melted butter. Add a little caster sugar to each one and turn to coat the buttery surfaces with sugar.

Melt the 45g of butter in a pan and add the plain flour and cornflour. Cook for a minute, stirring with a balloon whisk, then take the pan off the heat. Gradually add the milk, stirring after each addition to make sure there are no lumps, then add 50g of the sugar. Put the pan back on the heat and bring to the boil, stirring constantly, then cook for 3–4 minutes until the mixture has thickened. Remove the pan from the heat and stir in the lemon zest and juice, then the lightly beaten egg yolks. Allow the mixture to cool.

In a separate clean bowl, whisk the egg whites to soft peaks. Add the remaining 20g of sugar and continue to whisk until thick and glossy. Mix a large spoonful of the egg whites into the custard mixture to loosen it, then carefully fold in the rest, retaining as much volume as possible.

Spoon the mixture into the prepared ramekins. Run the handle of a spoon round the edge of each ramekin to loosen the mixture and allow the soufflés to rise with a nice 'top hat' effect. Immediately transfer them to the preheated baking sheet in the oven. Cook for 15–20 minutes until well risen, lightly golden and just set. Serve at once dusted with a little icing sugar, if using, with the sorbet on the side.

How much more delicate does the word tuiles sound than 'tile'? But perhaps it's just me and my lifelong love affair with the French language of food. The word actually refers to the curved terracotta tiles of Provence but even the image there is romantic. These crisp, light biscuits can be draped over a rolling pin and left to cool to give the traditional curled shape or made as flat discs.

ALMOND TUILES

MAKES ABOUT 20

50g unsalted butter
2 egg whites
100g caster sugar
55g plain flour
Pinch of salt
½ tsp almond extract
25g flaked almonds

Preheat the oven to 190°C/Fan 170°C. Line 3 baking sheets with baking parchment. Melt the butter in a small pan and set it aside to cool.

Whisk the egg whites until frothy and foamy. Add the sugar, 50g at a time, whisking well after each addition until the mixture is slightly thickened and well combined. Sift over the flour and salt and fold them in with the cooled melted butter and the almond extract.

Place teaspoonfuls of the mixture on the prepared baking sheets, leaving at least 12cm in between each one, as they will spread. Sprinkle a few flaked almonds on top of each biscuit.

Bake for 6-7 minutes, until golden brown. Remove the biscuits from the oven and transfer them to a wire rack to cool. Or, if you want to create the distinctive tuile curled shape, drape the biscuits over lightly greased rolling pins or wine bottles as soon as you take them out of the oven, then leave to cool completely.

Store the biscuits in an airtight tin or bag until ready to serve.

Not to be confused with the meringue-based macarons, these are small round biscuits made from almond paste and honey. In recent years, everyone has gone mad about the other macarons in pastel shades, but these little biscuits with a cup of tea or coffee in the afternoon are also exceptionally good. Can one ever get fed up with the taste of ground almonds in a confection?

ALMOND BISCUITS
MACARONS D'AMIENS

MAKES ABOUT 18

250g ground almonds
200g golden caster sugar
1 tbsp runny honey
1 tbsp apricot jam or
    apple or quince jelly
2 eggs, separated
1 tsp almond or
    vanilla extract

Mix the ground almonds, caster sugar, honey, jam or jelly, one of the egg yolks and the almond or vanilla extract in a bowl.

Lightly beat the egg whites and add enough of them to create a stiff dough like pastry or marzipan. Roll this into a 4cm diameter sausage, wrap it in cling film or baking parchment and seal the ends. Leave it to rest in the fridge until cool and firm.

Preheat the oven to 170°C/Fan 150°C. Line a baking tray with baking parchment. Cut the 'sausage' into 1.5cm thick rounds and place them on the baking tray, leaving a little space in between each one. Brush the top of each biscuit with the remaining egg yolk.

Bake the biscuits for 18–20 minutes or until pale golden brown. Put them on a wire rack to cool, and then store them in an airtight tin.

I am a great fan of puddings that are light and not too calorific but curiously, as it's one of my favourite sweets, I have never done a recipe for îles flottantes before. Roasting the rhubarb is a great way of preserving its shape and colour, even though it is properly cooked through.

FLOATING ISLANDS WITH ROASTED RHUBARB

ÎLES FLOTTANTES

SERVES 4

300g rhubarb,
    cut into 3cm lengths
70g golden caster sugar
Zest of 1 orange
1 tbsp orange juice
30g flaked almonds,
    toasted

Crème anglaise
500ml whole milk
1 vanilla pod, split
    lengthways and
    seeds scraped out
4 egg yolks
1 tsp cornflour
35g caster sugar

Meringues
2 egg whites
50g caster sugar
Pinch of fine salt

Preheat the oven to 200°C/Fan 180°C. Mix the rhubarb with the sugar, orange zest and juice, then tip it into a baking tray. Roast for 10–12 minutes until the rhubarb is tender but still holding its shape. Set aside and leave it to cool completely.

For the crème anglaise, pour the milk into a pan, add the vanilla pod and heat to just below boiling point. Remove the pan from the heat and allow the milk to cool and infuse for 10 minutes. Remove the vanilla pod and rinse and dry it, then add it to a jar of sugar to make vanilla sugar. Pour the infused milk into a bowl and rinse and dry the pan.

Mix the egg yolks with the cornflour and sugar in a separate bowl. Gradually add the milk, stirring all the time, and then pour the mixture into the clean pan. Place the pan over a low heat (it must be low or you risk scrambling the eggs) and keep stirring while the mixture thickens; it should coat the back of a spoon. Pour the mixture into a bowl and set it aside to cool, then put it in the fridge until ready to serve.

Set a wide shallow pan of water over a medium heat. Bring the water to a gentle simmer.

Whisk the egg whites in a clean bowl until they form soft, glossy peaks. Add a third of the sugar and whisk until incorporated, then repeat to add the remaining sugar in 2 batches.

Using a couple of serving spoons, shape the meringue mixture into 4 ovals and drop them into the poaching water. Cook for 2 minutes, then turn them over and continue to cook for 2 minutes on the other side. With a slotted spoon, transfer the meringues to a plate lined with kitchen paper.

Divide the crème anglaise between 4 bowls and place a meringue in the middle of each. Dot with pieces of the rhubarb and scatter with toasted flaked almonds, then serve at once.

A dacquoise is a kind of cake made with layers of meringue and is named after the town of Dax, near Bayonne in the Landes. I have to confess I have included a chocolate dacquoise in a previous book but I wanted to do a coffee version, as it is one of my favourite French dishes. It's the combination of crispness, nuttiness and creaminess that appeals to me. As I mentioned in the introduction to this chapter, making a dacquoise is a lot of work, and to someone a little prone to dessert disasters like me, the words of Julia Child, the great American cook of all things French, are a comfort: 'The meringue layers break easily, but don't worry if they do; breaks – or San Andreas faults – can be disguised... If it is irreparably cracked, too much so to be disguised with sugar, ice it with butter cream and later sprinkle with almonds.' Incidentally, dacquoise doesn't stay crisp for very long, but if you've got any leftover, put it in an ice cream machine with extra cream and it will give the luxury ice cream brands a run for their money!

COFFEE, ALMOND & HAZELNUT MERINGUE
DACQUOISE

SERVES 8

Meringue
75g blanched
   hazelnuts, toasted
4 egg whites
Pinch of fine salt
225g caster sugar

Coffee filling
400g whole milk
2 tbsp strong instant
   coffee powder
2 egg yolks
75g caster sugar
40g cornflour
100ml double cream

Chocolate ganache
150ml double cream
150g dark chocolate,
   chopped

Hazelnut praline
Vegetable oil,
   for greasing
100g sugar
1 tsp lemon juice
50g toasted blanched
   hazelnuts

First make the meringue. Pulse the hazelnuts in a food processor until they resemble fine breadcrumbs. Whisk the egg whites with the salt until fairly stiff. Add half the sugar and whisk again until glossy and stiff. Gently whisk in the remaining sugar to combine, then fold in the hazelnuts.

Preheat the oven to 110°C/Fan 90°C. Line baking sheets with baking parchment, then draw 3 x 20cm circles. Divide the meringue mixture between the 3 circles, then place them in the oven and bake for 1½–2 hours until the meringue is dry and crisp. Switch the oven off and leave the meringues to cool in the oven.

For the coffee filling, pour all but 3 tablespoons of the milk into a pan. Bring to the boil, then stir in the instant coffee. Mix the egg yolks and sugar in a bowl. Mix the cornflour with the remaining milk in a separate bowl, then stir this into the egg yolk mixture. Slowly add the hot milk, whisking continually to prevent lumps forming. Rinse out the milk pan, then pour in the mixture and whisk continuously over the heat until it comes to the boil. Lower the heat so the mixture just simmers, then stir for a couple of minutes until it is thickened and smooth. Directly cover the surface with cling film or baking parchment to prevent a skin forming and set it aside to cool for about an hour.

Whip the cream to soft peak stage and then whisk it into the coffee mixture. It will have set quite firm but will recover when whisked. Cover and refrigerate until needed.

To make the chocolate ganache, pour the cream into a pan and heat until it is almost boiling. Put the chopped chocolate in a bowl, then pour over the hot cream. Leave for 2 minutes, then stir until all the chocolate has melted and combined with the cream to make a thick glossy mixture. Set aside to cool.

Now make the praline. Lightly grease a baking sheet with vegetable oil or line it with baking parchment. Heat the sugar and lemon juice with a tablespoon of water in a pan over a medium heat. Once the sugar has dissolved, keep heating the mixture for 6–8 minutes until it turns a deep golden colour – keep a close eye on it and don't let it burn. Add the nuts, then immediately pour the mixture on to the baking sheet. When the praline is cool, transfer it to a food processor and pulse to coarse crumbs. Store in an airtight jar until ready to use.

Assemble the dacquoise just before serving. Place one of the meringues on a baking sheet and spread with half the coffee filling. Cover with a second disc and spread with the remaining filling, then top with the third disc. Spread the ganache around the sides of the dacquoise. Scatter the praline around it and then use a wide-bladed knife to push the praline up and over the sides of the cake. Serve at once.

Were you looking for an alternative to Christmas pudding this would be perfection. Not only is it similarly flavoured but it's also set in a traditional mould, so looks like a festive wreath. And being largely ice cream, it's a little less heavy than Christmas pudding but still very rich and celebratory. Legend has it that it was made popular in France by Maurice, the father of Christine Ferber the famous jam maker in Alsace. He wouldn't even write down his recipe for his daughter – she needed to make it her own – but I think once you have tasted it you get the general idea. Rich ice cream, lots of fruit macerated in Kirsch or Cognac, vanilla and orange zest. It is completely delicious and of course you can make it in advance. You will need a 22cm non-stick kougelhopf pan or bundt tin.

KOUGELHOPF GLACÉ

SERVES 8–10

100g raisins
75ml Kirsch or Cognac
3 eggs, separated
150g icing sugar
Zest of 1 large orange
2 vanilla pods, split
    lengthwise and seeds
    scraped out or 1 tsp
    vanilla paste or extract
2 whole eggs
650ml double cream
Pinch of salt
Butter, for greasing

To decorate
1–1½ tbsp cocoa
    powder, sifted
8–10 blanched or
    2 tbsp flaked
    almonds, toasted

Mix the raisins with the Kirsch or Cognac in a small bowl, then cover and leave them to macerate for 4–6 hours.

Put the 3 egg yolks, icing sugar, orange zest and vanilla seeds, paste or extract in a bowl, then crack in the whole eggs. Place the bowl over a pan of just simmering water and whisk until the mixture is pale, thickened and creamy. Now set the bowl over a pan of very cold water and continue to whisk until the mixture has cooled.

In a separate bowl, whip the cream and fold it into the cooled custard mixture. Wash the whisk blades and then whisk the egg whites with the salt in a clean bowl until you have soft peaks that hold their shape but are not dry. Add a little of the egg white to the custard mixture to loosen it, then fold in the rest so you have a light creamy custard.

Spoon the mixture into a plastic box and put it in the freezer for 1–2 hours to start to firm up. Remove it, fold in the soaked raisins and then pour into the lightly buttered kougelhopf pan or bundt tin. Cover with cling film and put it in the freezer for at least 12 hours.

Before serving, transfer the mould to the fridge for about 15 minutes to make it easier to turn out. Submerge the tin in tepid water a few times to loosen the kougelhopf and then upturn it on a serving plate. Put it back in the freezer for at least an hour to firm up and then transfer it to the fridge for 10 minutes before serving. Decorate with sifted cocoa powder and toasted blanched or flaked almonds.

My mother used to make this very simple recipe from Elizabeth David's *French Provincial Cooking*. Just two or three ingredients: dark chocolate, eggs and a perhaps a dash of coffee, orange juice or liqueur. The darker the chocolate the more bitter the mousse. Made with 70 per cent chocolate and espresso coffee, this is a dessert for the grown-ups. To quote from Julia Child again: 'I, for one, would much rather swoon over a few thin slices of prime beefsteak, or one small serving of chocolate mousse, or a sliver of foie gras than indulge to the full on such nonentities as fat-free gelatin puddings'. Gosh, I wish I'd met her.

CHOCOLATE MOUSSE
MOUSSE AU CHOCOLAT

SERVES 4

120g dark chocolate, 55–70%
   cocoa solids, chopped
1 tbsp espresso coffee,
   orange juice or rum,
   Cointreau or Grand
   Marnier (optional)
4 eggs, separated

To serve
20g grated dark chocolate
4 tsp full-fat crème fraiche
   or whipped cream

Put the chocolate and the coffee, juice or alcohol, if using, in a bowl and set it over a pan of just simmering water. Allow the chocolate to melt gently, then remove the bowl from the heat. Lightly beat the egg yolks and stir them into the chocolate.

In a separate bowl whisk the egg whites to glossy peaks. Mix in a spoonful of egg white into chocolate to loosen the mixture, then fold in the remaining egg whites. Make sure they are fully incorporated with no pockets of white left, while keeping as much air in the mixture as possible.

Spoon the mixture into 4 serving glasses, then cover and refrigerate for at least 4 hours to set.

Add a teaspoon of crème fraiche or whipped cream and a little grated chocolate to each one before serving.

Christine Ferber's jams are famous all over the world; they are expensive but do seem to have the edge over any other kind. I asked her what was so special about her jams and she swears by using untinned copper pans for some chemical reaction that helps the set. She doesn't add pectin and she's very particular about using only a few varieties of berry; her preferred strawberry is a small, very sweet variety called Corona. The other special points about her strawberry jam are that she uses a minute amount of vanilla, which is almost, but not quite, indiscernible, and finally the jam has to be not too firmly set. I really enjoyed my morning with Christine. She genuinely sticks to her principles but is also perfectly aware that with her amiable warm personality she could sell ice in the Arctic. I have to admit, though, that whatever variety of strawberries I tried I couldn't quite get the set that she achieved, so I have used jam sugar with pectin because the main thing is to cook the strawberries for as little time as possible and get a very soft set. This is my version of Christine's jam, and the raspberry tart on page 279 was inspired by the ones on sale in her shop.

SOFT-SET STRAWBERRY JAM

MAKES ABOUT 4 JARS

1.3kg fresh ripe strawberries, hulled and halved or quartered depending on size
1kg jam sugar (with added pectin)
25ml freshly squeezed lemon juice
1 vanilla pod, split and seeds scraped out

Place the chopped strawberries in a bowl with the jam sugar and vanilla seeds and pod and stir well to coat the strawberries. Cover and leave to macerate for 3-4 hours, stirring occasionally. After this time the strawberries should have released some of their liquid. Put a few saucers in the freezer for checking the set of the jam later.

Transfer the contents of the bowl to a large wide pan, preferably one with sloping sides, and gently warm the strawberries to dissolve the sugar. Once the sugar has liquified, turn up the heat, add the lemon juice and bring up to a rapid boil for about 10 minutes. Drop a teaspoon of the jam on to one of the cold saucers and allow it to cool for a minute. The jam is ready if there is a slight wrinkle when you push it with your finger. If not, boil for a little longer. Pour into sterilised jars. Serve with gâteau battu (page 295), toast, pancakes or waffles.

To sterilise jars, wash them in hot soapy water, then rinse and put them in the oven at 140°C for 20 minutes. Soak the lids in a bowl of boiling water, then drain and allow to air dry.

Confiture De Prune
Confiture de
Confiture d'abricot
Confiture de poire
Confiture de Prune
Confiture de Framboise

This recipe comes from La Colombe d'Or, a restaurant in Saint-Paul-de-Vence. It's more of a semifreddo than a vacherin, which is a meringue cake, but who am I to argue? It's been on their menu since at least the 1950s, when Paul Roux, founder of the restaurant and artist, painted the menu; the dishes have remained the same ever since. It is quite a time-consuming dish to prepare, as there are many stages to it, but it is absolutely worth the effort. All of it can be made the day before, so it's a great dinner party dessert. Or, if you like, you could save time and use bought vanilla ice cream and/or raspberry sorbet. The raspberry sorbet is delicious served with almond tuiles (page 262, or the lemon soufflés (page 258). *Recipe photograph overleaf.*

LA COLOMBE D'OR RASPBERRY VACHERIN SEMIFREDDO

SERVES 8

Ice cream
500ml double cream
100ml whole milk
1 vanilla pod, split,
    and seeds scraped out
90g caster sugar
5 egg yolks

Raspberry sorbet
120g caster sugar
1 tbsp liquid glucose
300g frozen raspberries
Juice of ½ lemon

Meringue
4 egg whites
Pinch of fine salt
200g caster sugar
Seeds of a vanilla pod
180g icing sugar sifted
    with 2 level tbsp cornflour

To serve
Fresh raspberries

First make the ice cream. Put the cream, milk and vanilla pod and seeds in a pan and place over a medium-high heat. Bring to the boil, then turn off the heat and leave to infuse.

Whisk the caster sugar and egg yolks in a large bowl until pale and thick. Remove the vanilla pod from the pan of cream and milk and gradually pour the warm mixture into the bowl of egg yolks and sugar, whisking constantly. Rinse out the pan and pour the mixture back in, then place over a low heat, stirring frequently with a wooden spoon. The custard will thicken in 5–6 minutes and should coat the back of a wooden spoon. Cover the surface with cling film or baking parchment and set it aside to cool completely, then put it in the fridge to chill. When the mixture is cold, transfer it to an ice cream maker and churn. Scoop into a freezerproof container and freeze until needed.

For the sorbet, heat 60ml of water in a pan with the caster sugar and liquid glucose. When it comes to a boil, remove the pan from the heat. Put the frozen raspberries in a food processor, pour over the hot liquid and the lemon juice and blitz until smooth.

Pour the mixture into a fine sieve over a bowl and push it through with a wooden spoon. Discard the seeds. Pour the sieved mixture into an ice cream maker and churn until smooth and semi-frozen. Transfer to a freezerproof container and freeze until needed.

Preheat the oven to 120°C/Fan 100°C. For the meringue, whisk the whites with the salt until they form soft peaks. Add the caster sugar a little at a time and whisk to thick, glossy peaks. Fold in the vanilla seeds and the sifted icing sugar and cornflour.

You will need a terrine or loaf tin measuring about 23 x 13cm for assembling the dish. Line 2 baking trays with baking parchment. Measure the base of your terrine or tin and draw 2 rectangles of that size on each piece of baking parchment. Spread a layer of meringue about 1cm thick over each rectangle. If you have any meringue left over, spread it on a separate baking sheet; cooked meringue keeps for a week in an airtight container. Bake the meringue for 1½ hours, then switch off the oven and leave the meringue to cool completely.

Remove the ice cream and sorbet from the freezer to soften slightly. Line the terrine or loaf tin with baking parchment or cling film and trim the meringue rectangles to fit if necessary.

Place a rectangle of meringue in the lined tin and cover with a layer of ice cream 1cm thick. Gently place another rectangle of meringue on top and spread with a layer of raspberry sorbet 1cm thick. Add a third rectangle of meringue and spread with more ice cream, then finish with the final layer of meringue. Cover well and freeze for 12 hours or overnight.

To serve, briefly dip the tin in a basin of warm water to release the vacherin. Cut into thick slices with a hot, wet knife and serve at once on chilled plates with fresh raspberries.

If you prefer, you could use a round springform tin. Just measure the diameter, draw out rounds on the parchment and proceed as above.

This comes from Christine Ferber's pastry shop, Maison Ferber, in the Alsace village of Niedermorschwihr. Now try to pronounce that! Such tarts are the sort of thing that delights the eye as you gaze through the shop window.

FRENCH RASPBERRY TART

TARTE AUX FRAMBOISES

SERVES 8

Sweet pastry
85g softened butter
85g caster sugar
3 egg yolks
175g plain flour, sifted

Crème patissière
250ml whole milk
1 vanilla pod, split,
    and seeds scraped out
3 egg yolks
50g caster sugar
10g plain flour
10g cornflour

To decorate
400g fresh raspberries
5 tbsp redcurrant jelly

To serve
Whipped cream

For the pastry, mix the butter and sugar in a bowl, then add the egg yolks to make a smooth paste. Add the flour and mix to bring the dough together in a ball. Wrap it in cling film and chill for up to 20–30 minutes until firm enough to roll.

For the crème patissière, bring the milk to the boil with the vanilla pod and seeds, then remove the pan from the heat. Mix the egg yolks, sugar and both flours in a bowl to form a paste.

Gradually add the warm milk to the egg and flour paste, removing the vanilla pod, and stir well until you have a smooth custard. Rinse out the milk pan and pour in the custard mixture. Bring it to the boil over a medium heat and stir continuously, until the custard is really thick. Remove the pan from the heat. Cover the surface of the crème patissière with cling film or greaseproof paper, then set aside to cool.

Preheat the oven to 190°C/Fan 170°C. Roll out the pastry and use it to line a loose-bottomed 25cm tart tin or 8 individual 10cm loose-bottomed tart tins. Line the pastry with greaseproof paper and add baking beans, then bake for 10 minutes. Remove the paper and beans and put the pastry back in the oven for another 4–5 minutes to finish cooking. Set aside to cool.

Carefully remove the pastry from the tin or tins and fill with the chilled crème patissière. Smooth the top with a damp palette knife. Arrange the raspberries on top in concentric circles. Warm the redcurrant jelly in a pan with a tablespoon of water. Using a pastry brush, generously paint the raspberries with the warm jelly, then leave to set. Serve with whipped cream.

You would expect to find a really good walnut tart in the city of Périgueux, as every second tree in Périgord seems to be a walnut, and indeed I did in a little place in the centre of the city called Le Relais Périgourdin. The filling of this is very simple, just a caramel with large chunks of walnut, honey, crème fraiche and egg yolks.

WALNUT TART FROM PÉRIGORD

TARTE AUX NOIX MAISON

SERVES 8–10

Pastry
235g plain flour,
   plus extra for rolling
130g cold unsalted
   butter, diced
1½ tbsp caster sugar
Pinch salt
2 tbsp ice-cold water

Filling
100g granulated sugar
230g walnut pieces,
   roughly chopped
3 tbsp clear honey
300g full-fat crème fraiche
3 egg yolks

To serve
Crème fraiche or ice cream

Pulse the flour, butter, sugar and salt in a food processor until the mixture resembles breadcrumbs. Tip the mixture into a bowl and add as much of the cold water as required to bring the dough together. Wrap it in cling film and leave it to rest for 10 minutes in the fridge.

Roll out the pastry on a lightly floured board and use it to line a 25cm loose-bottomed shallow tart tin. Cover and chill in the fridge or freezer for at least 30 minutes.

Preheat the oven to 180°C/Fan 160°C. Put the sugar in a pan with about 60ml of water and place over a low heat until the sugar has dissolved. Turn up the heat and cook until it turns golden-brown.

Remove the pan from the heat and stir in the nuts, honey, crème fraiche and egg yolks. Mix well, then pour into the chilled pastry case and bake for about 30 minutes. Allow to cool to warm or room temperature and serve with crème fraiche or ice cream.

This is a celebration of the apricots I saw in Périgueux market in early September. There can't be a better time to visit such a market. Peaches were still in abundance, as well as boxes of ripe plums, reines claudes, which we know as greengages, misshapen apples with their leaves still on the stalks, and boxes of pale golden muscat grapes, but the apricots were particularly glorious in their orange skins sometimes blushed with red. Ever since reading Webster's *The Duchess of Malfi* for O-Level, I've associated apricots with sensuousness. The duchess is secretly pregnant and greedy for them. '...her tetchiness, and most vulturous eating of the apricocks, are apparent signs of breeding', says the malcontent Bosola. I do a lot of tarts like this one because of the ease of ready-made all-butter puff pastry. Here, I have just put some ground almonds in the base to absorb the juice which will come out of the fruits when baking, then dusted the apricots with icing sugar before they go in the oven to caramelise. The tart is finished with a glaze of warm sieved apricot jam. Cold crème fraiche is the only accompaniment to this. *Recipe photograph overleaf.*

APRICOT TART

TARTE FINE AUX ABRICOTS

SERVES 6–8

275g all-butter puff pastry
4 tbsp ground almonds
450g fresh ripe apricots,
    stoned and cut in
    halves or quarters,
    depending on size
    (or use tinned apricots)
2 tbsp icing sugar
6–8 tbsp apricot jam

To serve
Crème fraiche

Preheat the oven to 200°C/Fan 180°C. Roll out the pastry into a long bar shape measuring about 15 x 35–40cm and transfer it to a baking sheet. With a sharp knife, score all around the pastry about 1.5cm in from the edge, but take care not to cut all the way through to the base. You just want to allow a border to rise around the fruit.

Sprinkle the ground almonds over the pastry within the score lines. Arrange the apricots, cut side up, over the ground almonds, keeping them tightly packed. Dust the apricots with the icing sugar.

Bake the tart for 25–30 minutes until the apricots are tender and caramelised and the pastry is risen and golden. Allow to cool to room temperature.

Warm the apricot jam over a low heat, then pass it through a sieve before brushing it liberally over the tart to glaze. Serve with crème fraiche.

I was so taken with the savoury tarte flambée (page 83) that I thought I would try making a sweet version incorporating the idea of a French tarte fine but adding a topping of the much-loved crumble. It's not one of those irritating crumble tops you get in posh restaurants that are sprinkled on at the last minute; it's baked on the tart and is, dare I say it myself, remarkably good. This is the sort of thing I will often resort to if I've got a few people round. You can have it all prepped, ready to bake when your guests arrive.

TARTE FLAMBÉE WITH APPLES

SERVES 6

Dough
125g plain flour, sifted, plus extra for rolling
¼ tsp salt
80ml tepid water
1 tbsp sunflower oil

Crumble mix
40g plain flour
25g butter
15g sugar
10g hazelnuts, chopped

Apple topping
3–4 dessert apples, Coxes in season or Braeburns
20g butter, melted
2 tbsp icing sugar
¼ tsp ground cinnamon

To serve
Crème fraiche

For the dough, mix the flour and salt in a bowl, add the water and oil and bring together into a rough dough. Transfer the dough to a floured board and knead well. Roll it out into a circle about 28cm in diameter or a rectangle of about 35 x 23cm, then transfer it to a baking sheet.

Make the crumble topping by rubbing the flour and butter together in a bowl until the mixture resembles breadcrumbs. Stir in the sugar and hazelnuts. Core and slice the apples very thinly, leaving the skin on. Preheat the oven to 210°C/Fan 190°C.

Arrange the apple slices in overlapping circles or rows on the dough base. Brush them with the melted butter and sprinkle over the icing sugar mixed with the cinnamon. Sprinkle the crumble topping over the apples.

Bake in the preheated oven for 15–18 minutes or until the base is crisp and the apples and crumble topping are golden. Transfer to a wooden board and cut into slices. Serve with crème fraiche.

I had a generous slice of this prune tart in the village of Trizac in the Auvergne, mostly because it looked so classically rustic French and is unlike any other fruit tart. There's nothing in it other than prunes and pastry, and a slice of this with crème fraiche is pretty special. It's interesting to learn why Agen prunes are so much a part of the cuisine of the Auvergne, which doesn't really lend itself to the growing of plums. It's simply because, traditionally, barges would come up the Dordogne river, trading prunes from the south for Auvergne timber and cheese.

AGEN PRUNE TART

TARTE AUX PRUNEAUX D'AGEN

SERVES 8

800g large Agen prunes
  (semi-dried), pitted
250g plain flour, sifted,
  plus extra for rolling
1 tsp baking powder, sifted
60g caster sugar
½ tsp salt
125g unsalted butter, at room
  temperature, cubed
1 egg, beaten
1–2 tbsp ice-cold water

Put the prunes in a pan and just cover them with water. Cook over a low heat, stirring often, until the mixture has a jammy consistency; this should take 20–30 minutes. Leave the mixture to cool.

Put the flour, baking powder, sugar and salt in a food processor, add the cubes of butter and pulse until the mixture resembles breadcrumbs. Transfer it to a bowl and add about half the beaten egg, mixed with a tablespoon of the water – just enough to bring the dough together. Add the additional water if required. Reserve the rest of the egg for brushing the pastry.

Cut the dough into three-quarters and a quarter. On a floured work surface, roll out the larger piece to a circle about 35cm in diameter and 3–4mm thick and trim the edges. Place it on a baking sheet.

Roll out the remaining pastry into a rectangle about 25cm long and cut 6–8 strips, about 1cm wide. Spread the prune 'jam' over the pastry disc, leaving a 4–5cm border around the edge. Place half the dough strips over the prunes in one direction, spacing them evenly. Then lay the remaining strips in the opposite direction at right angles to form a lattice.

Fold the sides of the base up and over the edges of the lattice strips. Neaten the edges and brush the pastry with the remaining beaten egg. Put the tart in the fridge to chill while the oven heats up.

Preheat the oven to 210°C/Fan 190°C. Bake the tart for 30–40 minutes until the pastry is a deep golden colour.

To be honest, I'm always looking at slightly more elaborate ways of serving up strawberries and cream because, left to my own devices, I wouldn't order anything else in the summer when strawberries are perfect. And for me, the combination of sablé biscuits with strawberries and vanilla cream is perfection. Is there anything more French than the crisp, buttery sandiness of sablés? The recipe below makes more than you need for the strawberries, so store the rest in an airtight tin; they're delicious with a cup of tea.

STRAWBERRIES & CREAM WITH VANILLA SUGAR & SABLÉ BISCUITS

SERVES 4

400g Sweet Eve strawberries
200ml double cream,
    lightly whipped
2 tbsp vanilla sugar

Sablé biscuits
200g unsalted butter
60g caster sugar
½ tsp vanilla extract
1 egg yolk
150g plain flour,
    plus extra for rolling
Pinch of salt
1 egg yolk, for glazing

Vanilla sugar
200g caster sugar
1 vanilla pod, split
    lengthways and
    seeds scraped out

For the biscuits, beat together the butter and sugar with the vanilla extract until pale and fluffy. Add the egg yolk and once incorporated, add the flour and salt and mix until the mixture just comes together in a dough. Form it into a ball, flatten to about 2cm thick, then wrap in cling film and leave it in the fridge for about an hour to firm up.

Preheat the oven to 190°C/Fan 170°C. Line a couple of baking trays with baking parchment. Roll the dough out on a floured board to about 4mm thick. Using an oval-shaped cutter measuring about 10cm long, cut the biscuits out and arrange them on the baking trays. You should have 16–20 biscuits. Brush the tops with the remaining egg yolk and bake for 12–15 minutes or until crisp and golden. Transfer the biscuits to a wire rack to cool completely.

To make the vanilla sugar, put the caster sugar in a food processor and add the vanilla seeds. Pulse to distribute them well, then pour the sugar into a preserving jar with the pods and seal. The sugar keeps for months if well sealed.

Serve the strawberries and cream with the vanilla sugar and sablé biscuits.

Cherries are far and away my favourite fruit – for me, there's no contest – and whenever we were in a town with a market last May and June I had to buy a kilo. To be honest, I get disappointed with the crew when they don't share my enthusiam and greed. I have never thought of doing a recipe for clafoutis, but Portia Spooner, with whom I test recipes, insisted it was worth a try. I find that the problem with clafoutis, apart from why would you want to meddle with cherries, is that the batter when baked can become rather firm and rubbery, like a bad Yorkshire pudding. What Portia has done is to separate the eggs and fold the whisked egg whites in at the end. Suddenly the batter has a moussey lightness after baking and that really concentrates your attention on the cherries.

CHERRY CLAFOUTIS

SERVES 6

500g fresh cherries, washed, pitted and stalks removed (or use drained tinned or frozen pitted dark cherries)
80g caster sugar, plus extra for coating the dish
3 tbsp Kirsch, brandy or rum
20g butter, melted, plus extra to grease
55g plain flour
Pinch of salt
2 large eggs, separated
290ml whole milk
¼ tsp almond extract (optional)
2 tbsp flaked almonds, toasted
Icing sugar, for dusting

Put the cherries in a bowl and lightly crush them with the back of a wooden spoon so the skins break a little but the fruit retains its shape. Add 30g of the caster sugar and the alcohol, then stir and leave to macerate for an hour or two.

Preheat the oven to 200°C/Fan 180°C. Butter a baking dish measuring about 20 x 25cm and then add a tablespoon of the caster sugar. Turn the dish to coat the greased surfaces with a light dusting of sugar.

Sift the flour and salt into a mixing bowl and add the remaining 50g of caster sugar. Make a well in the centre and then whisk in the egg yolks. Gradually add the milk, melted butter and almond extract to make a smooth batter, then add the cherries and their macerating liquid and stir well.

In a separate bowl, whisk the egg whites to soft peaks. Add a spoonful of the egg whites to the batter to loosen it, then fold in the remaining whites, keeping as much volume as possible.

Pour the mixture into the prepared baking dish and bake for about 35 minutes. The batter should be just set but with a slight wobble. Serve warm sprinkled with toasted almonds and a dusting of icing sugar. Some vanilla ice cream alongside is nice.

In Haut-Jura there is a restaurant called La Boissaude in Rochejean, way up in the foothills of the Alps. It's so high, in fact, that people are skiing all around in the winter. Their raison d'être is côte de boeuf grilled over a large open fire which I'm a complete sucker for, but they also do a fabulous bilberry tart. I don't know why bilberries are so hard to come by in this country; they're easy to grow, I think. But everyone grows blueberries, maybe because they are three times the size and easier to pick? I like to think the bilberries in the tart at La Boissaude were gathered wild from *Sound of Music*-type pastures and they certainly had a tangy, almost pine-like taste. I did test this recipe using blueberries, as you can get them everywhere, and it's still very nice, particularly because the tart is really stuffed with fruit, with a very light binding of egg custard. Another feature of this restaurant is that if you're lucky, you might get to enjoy a performance on the Alpine horn.

BILBERRY TART

TARTE AUX MYRTILLES

SERVES 8

Pastry
210g plain flour,
 plus extra for rolling
Pinch salt
100g cold butter, cubed
40g caster sugar
1 egg, beaten
1 tbsp ice-cold water

Filling
75g ground almonds
600g bilberries, stems
 removed, washed and
 dried (or use 600g fresh
 or frozen blueberries)
150ml double cream
75g icing sugar, sifted
2 eggs, beaten
1 tsp vanilla extract

To serve
Crème fraiche

For the pastry, put the flour, salt and butter in a food processor and pulse until the mixture resembles breadcrumbs. Transfer it to a bowl and stir in the sugar, then fold in the egg and enough of the water to bring everything together into a smooth non-sticky dough.

Wrap the dough in cling film and chill for about 20 minutes. Roll out the pastry on a lightly floured board to a circle measuring about 28cm in diameter. Use it to line a 25cm loose-bottomed tin and prick the base all over with a fork. Chill again in the fridge or freezer for 20–30 minutes.

Preheat the oven to 190°C/Fan 170°C. Line the pastry case with crumpled greaseproof paper and add some baking beans. Bake for about 10 minutes, then remove the paper and beans and put the pastry back in the oven for another 3–4 minutes to dry out the base. Turn the oven down to 180°C/Fan 160°C.

Sprinkle the pastry with ground almonds, then add the berries and bake for 15 minutes.

Meanwhile, make a custard by mixing the double cream, icing sugar, eggs and vanilla extract in a bowl. Pour this mixture over the berries and bake for another 30 minutes, or until the tart filling is fairly firm and golden.

Leave the tart to cool on a wire rack in the tin. Serve warm or at room temperature with cream or crème fraiche.

Buckwheat pancakes are particularly popular in Normandy and one of the nicest ways of eating them is spread with butterscotch apple caramel, Dieppe style. You can buy jars of this in Normandy, but it's easy to make your own.

BUCKWHEAT GALETTES WITH APPLE CARAMEL

MAKES ABOUT 8

Butterscotch apple caramel
350g cooking apples,
    peeled and cored,
    cut into 2.5cm chunks
110g unsalted butter
150g soft dark brown sugar
125ml double cream
¼ tsp sea salt flakes

Galettes
75g buckwheat flour
25g plain flour
Large pinch of salt
120ml whole milk,
    plus extra as required
2 eggs, beaten
25g melted butter,
    plus extra for cooking

To serve
30g butter
1 tbsp golden caster sugar
3-4 crisp eating apples,
    such as Braeburn
    cored and each cut
    into 8 wedges

To serve
Crème fraiche or ice cream

Put the chunks of cooking apple in a pan with a splash of water and cook until mushy. Blitz them to a smooth purée, then set aside. Melt the butter in a pan, then add the brown sugar and stir well until dissolved. Whisk in the cream and continue to cook for about 5 minutes over a medium heat. When the mixture has thickened, stir in the apple purée and season to taste with the sea salt. Serve immediately or pour into a large sterilised jam jar and refrigerate. It should last for a week in the fridge; just reheat as required.

For the galettes, put the flours and salt in a mixing bowl and whisk in the milk, eggs, melted butter and enough water to make a batter about the consistency of double cream. Leave to rest for 30 minutes.

Take a non-stick crêpe or frying pan about 25cm in diameter and brush the base with a little melted butter. Pour in a thin layer of the batter and swirl the pan so the mixture lightly coats the base. Cook over a fairly high heat for about 2 minutes until lightly browned. Flip the pancake over and cook on the other side. Slide it on to a warmed plate and keep it warm while you cook the rest of the galettes.

In a separate frying pan, heat the butter and caster sugar until dissolved. Add the wedges of eating apple and cook, turning them every now and then until they are softened and golden.

Warm the sauce and fold in two-thirds of the apple wedges. Fold the pancakes into triangles and spoon over the apple caramel. Serve with the remaining apple wedges and crème fraiche or ice cream.

Gâteau battu is from the Somme area of France. 'Battu' literally means beaten cake and it's traditionally baked in fluted metal moulds, but for ease I'm using a bundt tin. With its rich buttery yeasted batter, this cake is like a cross between a brioche and a panettone, not too sweet. It's extremely nice as it is, spread with the soft-set strawberry jam on page 271, toasted or even dipped in egg and fried in butter, like pain perdu.

GÂTEAU BATTU

MAKES ABOUT 8 SLICES

140g butter, melted,
    plus extra for greasing
3 tsp active dried yeast
4 tbsp warm milk
225g plain flour
½ tsp salt
50g golden caster sugar
4 large eggs, 2 whole
    and 2 separated

Generously butter a non-stick bundt tin measuring about 20cm in diameter and 10cm deep. Sprinkle the dried yeast over the warm milk in a jug and leave it somewhere warm to froth and foam for a few minutes.

Sift the flour, salt and sugar into a large bowl and make a well in the centre. Crack in the 2 whole eggs, then add 2 of the yolks, the melted butter and the frothy yeast mixture. Beat to make a smooth batter.

In a separate bowl whisk the 2 remaining egg whites to soft peaks. Beat a tablespoon of the egg whites into the batter to loosen it, then gently fold in the rest with a large metal spoon.

Turn the mixture into the greased tin and cover loosely with a clean tea towel or cling film. Leave the cake to rise in a warm place for about an hour or until doubled in size.

Preheat the oven to 190°C/Fan 170°C. Bake the cake for 25–30 minutes or until golden brown. Cool for a few minutes in the tin and then turn out on to a wire rack to finish cooling.

VEGETABLE STOCK
Makes about 2 litres

2 large onions, roughly chopped
2 large carrots, roughly chopped
1 head celery, roughly chopped
1 fennel bulb, roughly chopped
1 garlic bulb, split into cloves
3 bay leaves
1 tsp salt

Put everything in a large pan with 3 litres of water and bring to the boil. Simmer for an hour, then strain.

FISH STOCK
Makes about 1.2 litres

1kg fish heads, skin and bones
    (use any except oily fish
    like mackerel, sardines,
    herrings, salmon)
1 fennel bulb, roughly chopped
100g celery, chopped
100g carrots, roughly chopped
25g button mushrooms,
    quartered
1 thyme sprig

Put all the ingredients in a large pan with 2.5 litres of water and simmer gently for 30 minutes, then strain.

ROASTED FISH STOCK
Makes about 1.2 litres

25g butter
1kg fish heads, skin and bones
    (use any except oily fish
    like mackerel, sardines,
    herrings, salmon)
100g celery, roughly chopped
100g carrots, roughly chopped
1 thyme sprig

This stock has a slightly caramelised flavour and can be used for recipes where a stronger taste is required. Preheat the oven to 200°C/ Fan 180°C. Melt the butter in a large roasting tin. Add the fish bones, vegetables and thyme and turn them over a few times until they are all well coated in butter. Roast in the oven for

30 minutes, then transfer the mixture to a pan, add 2.5 litres of water and bring just to the boil. Simmer for 20 minutes and then strain into a clean pan. Bring back to the boil and boil until reduced to about 1.2 litres.

SHELLFISH STOCK/REDUCTION
Makes about 1 litre stock
    or 150ml reduction

15g unsalted butter
50g carrot, chopped
50g onion, chopped
50g celery, chopped
350g shell-on prawns
    (or shrimp or small crabs)
75ml white wine
A couple of tarragon sprigs
200ml tinned chopped tomatoes
1.2 litres fish stock
Pinch of cayenne pepper

Melt the butter in a large pan. Add the carrot, onion and celery and fry gently for 3–4 minutes until starting to soften. Add the prawns and fry for another 2 minutes, then add all the remaining ingredients, lower the heat and simmer for 40 minutes.
   Strain the stock, pressing out as much liquid as possible with the back of a ladle. This can now be used as a shellfish stock or reduced further for a much stronger-tasting reduction. For the reduction, bring the stock back to the boil and boil rapidly until you are left with about 150ml of liquid.

CHICKEN STOCK
Makes about 1.75 litres

Bones from a 1.5kg chicken
    or 450g wings or drumsticks
    or leftover bones from a
    roasted chicken
1 large carrot, roughly chopped
2 celery sticks, roughly chopped
2 leeks, sliced
2 bay leaves
2 thyme sprigs

Put all the ingredients in a pan with 2.25 litres of water and bring to the boil, then immediately turn down to a simmer. Skim off any scum from the surface, then leave the stock to simmer very gently for 2 hours – don't let it boil again as that emulsifies any fat and makes the stock cloudy. Strain and then simmer for a little longer to concentrate the flavour if desired.

BEEF STOCK
Makes about 2.4 litres

2 celery sticks, roughly chopped
2 carrots, roughly chopped
2 onions, roughly chopped
900g shin of beef or beef bones
5 litres water
2 bay leaves
2 thyme sprigs
1 tbsp salt

For a pale brown stock, put all the ingredients except the bay leaves, thyme and salt into a large pan, add 5 litres of water and bring to the boil. Skim off the scum that rises to the surface. Simmer for 3 hours adding the salt and herbs after 2½ hours. Strain the stock into a bowl or clean pan. For a richer-tasting stock, continue to cook and reduce the liquid.

RICH BEEF STOCK
Makes about 2.4 litres

2 tbsp vegetable oil
2 celery sticks, roughly chopped
2 carrots, roughly chopped
2 onions, roughly chopped
30g tomato purée
900g shin of beef or beef bones
1 tbsp salt
2 bay leaves
2 thyme sprigs

For a deep-flavoured, rich-coloured stock, heat the oil in the pan, add the vegetables, tomato purée and beef and fry for 10–15 minutes until nicely browned. Add 5 litres of water and bring to the boil. Turn down the heat, skim off any scum from the surface, then simmer for 3 hours adding the salt and herbs after 2½ hours. Top up with cold water if the level drops beneath the meat and vegetables. Strain the stock before using.

If using bones, roast them in a hot oven (220°C/Fan 200°C) for up to an hour until well browned. Brown the vegetables with the oil, as above, then add the bones and tomato purée and proceed as above.

GREEN PISTOU

A good bunch (about 50g) basil leaves
3 fat cloves garlic
1 ripe tomato, skinned and chopped
75g Parmesan cheese, grated
150ml olive oil
Salt and black pepper

Blend the basil, garlic and tomato and cheese together in a food processor. Then with the machine still running, gradually add the olive oil to make a pesto-like mixture. Season to taste with salt and pepper.

SUNDRIED TOMATO PISTOU

10 sundried tomatoes
1 clove garlic
30g Parmesan cheese, grated
90ml extra virgin olive oil
Salt and black pepper

Blend the sundried tomatoes with the garlic and cheese in a food processor. Then with the machine still running, gradually add the olive oil to make a pesto-like mixture. Season to taste with salt and pepper.

TOMATO SAUCE

1kg tomatoes, chopped, or 2 x 400g tins of chopped tomatoes
4 tbsp olive oil
5 garlic cloves, chopped
1 tsp herbes de Provence or a couple of thyme and rosemary sprigs
½ tsp sugar
Salt and black pepper

Combine all the ingredients in a pan and season with a teaspoon of salt and plenty of black pepper. Place over a very low heat, cover with a lid and leave to cook very slowly for 3–4 hours. Use immediately, or leave to cool and refrigerate or freeze.

VELOUTÉ SAUCE
Makes 600ml

600ml fish stock (page 301)
300ml milk
50g butter
50g plain flour

Pour the stock and milk into a pan and bring to the boil. In a separate pan, melt the butter, stir in the flour and cook for 2 minutes, stirring constantly without allowing the mixture to colour.

When it starts to smell nutty, add about a third of the milk and stock mixture and whisk or stir until thickened and smooth. Add another third and repeat and then the remaining third. Leave to simmer gently for about 30 minutes. If not using the sauce immediately, transfer it to a lidded container and allow it to cool. You can keep this indefinitely in the fridge if you reboil it every 5 days but it does not freeze well.

CLASSIC VINAIGRETTE

8 tsp rapeseed or sunflower oil
2 tsp white wine vinegar
¼ tsp salt
⅛ tsp sugar

Whisk everything together or put in a jar or plastic box and shake.

MUSTARD MAYONNAISE
Makes 300ml

1 egg
1 tbsp English mustard (made up, not powder)
1 tsp salt
1 tsp white wine vinegar
300ml sunflower oil

Blend the egg, mustard, salt and vinegar in a food processor. With the motor running, gradually add the sunflower oil in a slow trickle until it is all incorporated. Store in the fridge.

GARLIC-INFUSED OLIVE OIL

200ml olive oil
6 cloves garlic, peeled and bashed

Put the oil in a pan with the garlic and warm gently for 30 minutes. Leave to cool, then strain out the garlic. Store the oil in an airtight jar or bottle for up to a month for use in garlic-mashed potato and dressings.

CONFIT GARLIC

250–300ml olive oil
20–24 cloves garlic, peeled
A couple of thyme sprigs (optional)

Put the oil in a pan with the garlic and thyme, if using. Heat the oil to 100°C and poach the garlic for 45–60 minutes until softened, without allowing it to brown. Pour into sterilised jars and cool. This keeps well in the fridge for a couple of weeks.

CONFIT PORK SKIN

450g pork skin with 1cm
  of fat attached
100g salt
600g duck or goose fat or lard

Cut the pork skin into pieces
measuring 8 x 2cm. Salt all the
surfaces and put the salted
skin in a glass bowl or oven
dish. Cover well and leave
it in the fridge for 6 hours.

Preheat the oven to 140°C/
Fan 120°C. Rinse off the salt
and dry the skin. Put it in an
ovenproof dish, cover with a
lid or foil and cook for 2 hours.
Pack into sterilised jars and top
up with the liquid fat, then allow
to cool. Store it in the fridge
until needed; it should keep
for weeks or even months.

CONFIT DUCK LEGS

4 large duck legs
100g salt
4 thyme sprigs
900g duck or goose fat

Make the duck confit at least
24 hours before you want to
use it in a dish. Place 1 duck leg
in the bottom of a deep plastic,
glass or stainless steel bowl.
Sprinkle with a little of the salt,
turn the duck over and sprinkle
with more salt. Repeat with the
remaining duck legs and salt.
Cover and leave in the fridge
for 6 hours, turning the legs
over after 3 hours. Don't leave
the duck any longer or it will
be too salty.

Preheat the oven to 140°C/
Fan 120°C. Rinse the salt off
the duck legs and put them
and the thyme in a flameproof
casserole dish in which they fit
snugly. Melt the duck or goose
fat and pour it over the legs,
making sure they are completely
covered. Cover the dish with
a lid and put it in the oven for
1½ hours. Remove and allow
the duck legs to cool in the fat.

MELBA TOAST

Toast medium thick slices of
white bread under a grill until
lightly golden on both sides.
Transfer them to a board
and cut off the crusts.

Put your hand on each slice
and run a knife horizontally
through the doughy middle
of the bread separating the
2 toasted sides. Cut each slice
into 2 triangles and grill the
uncooked side until crisp and
golden. Cool and serve with
duck liver parfait (page 170)
or with other pâtés or cheese.

CROUTONS

2 slices slightly stale white
  bread, crusts removed
3 tbsp olive oil
Salt

Preheat the oven to 180°C/
Fan 160°C. Cut the bread into
cubes of about 2cm. Toss them
with the oil in a bowl until lightly
coated, then season with salt.
Scatter them on a baking tray
and bake for 8–10 minutes until
golden and crisp. Use immediately
or allow to cool and keep in an
airtight container for a day or
so. Refresh them in a hot oven
for a minute or so before using.
You can also make a more
rugged version by cutting slices
of sourdough bread, crusts and
all, into 2cm pieces.

BEURRE MANIÉ

Blend equal quantities of
softened butter and plain flour
together to form a smooth paste.
Cover and keep in the fridge
until needed. This will keep for
same length of time as butter.

CLARIFIED BUTTER

Place the butter in a small pan
and leave it over a very low heat
until it has melted. Then skim
off any scum from the surface
and pour off the clear (clarified)
butter into a bowl, leaving
behind the milky white solids
that will have settled on the
bottom of the pan.

BOUQUET GARNI

12cm celery stick
8 parsley sprigs (with stalks)
5 thyme sprigs on stalks
1 bay leaf

Tuck the herbs into the groove in
the celery stalk and tie up tightly
with kitchen string. Use to flavour
soups and stews.

RICK'S PEPPERMIX

1 chipotle chilli, seeds removed
1 pasilla chilli, seeds removed
  (see suppliers, page 309)
2 tbsp black peppercorns
2 tbsp white peppercorns
2 tsp Szechuan peppercorns
1 tbsp salt

Blitz all the ingredients
together in a spice grinder.

PILAF RICE

1 small shallot, finely chopped
1 tsp butter
1 bay leaf
150g short-grain paella rice
½ tsp salt

Fry the shallot gently in the
butter with the bay leaf in a small
saucepan. Add the rice and salt,
then stir. Pour in 180ml of water,
bring to the boil, then cover and
turn the heat down to a very low
simmer. Simmer for 10 minutes,
then leave with the heat off
for another 3 minutes.

COOK'S TIPS

I like my recipes to be as easy to use as possible. Generally, I don't specify the weight of garlic cloves, tomatoes, carrots or onions because the reality of cooking is you just take a clove or two of garlic or a whole onion. However, I thought it would be sensible to suggest the weights (unpeeled) that I have in mind:

1 garlic clove: 5g
1 small onion: 100g
1 medium onion: 175g
1 large onion: 225g
Small handful fresh herbs: about 15g
Large handful fresh herbs: about 30g

All teaspoon and tablespoon measurements are level unless otherwise stated and are based on measuring spoons:

1 teaspoon = 5ml
1 tablespoon = 15ml

Readers in Australia need to make minor adjustments, as their tablespoon measure is 20ml.

OVEN TEMPERATURES
We have given settings for regular and fan ovens throughout the book. Should you need gas settings, they are as follows:

°C	°C FAN	GAS
120	100	½
140	120	1
150	130	2
160	140	3
180	160	4
190	170	5
200	180	6
220	200	7
230	210	8
240	220	9

EGGS
Use medium free-range eggs in the recipes, unless otherwise specified.

FINES HERBES
The French use this combination of fresh herbs most frequently in light egg or fish dishes or in soups or salads. Classically, it means a combination of equal quantities of chervil, tarragon, chives and parsley, but you can use just two or three of these if not all are available.

PIMENT D'ESPELETTE
This red chilli pepper from the Pays Basque is spicy but quite mild compared to other chillies. Piment d'Espelette is available in good spice shops or online and due to its rarity is comparatively expensive. If unavailable, substitute hot (unsmoked) paprika, chilli flakes or pimentón picante, which will give a more Catalonian flavour. I've suggested suitable substitutions wherever the piment is used.

COOKING LIVE LOBSTER
First put the lobster in the freezer for at least 2 hours to render it unconscious. Fill a large pan with 4 litres of water and 170g of salt and bring to the boil. Add the lobster and poach for 12 minutes. Remove it from the water and leave it until cool enough to handle.

SUPPLIERS

Ingredients for the photography in this book were sourced from the following retailers:

Amazon www.amazon.co.uk
Piment d'Espelette, Kampot pepper, Wayanad pepper, snails, Montbéliarde sausages, Banyuls vinegar, dashi stock, brik pastry

French Click www.frenchclick.co.uk
Piment d'Espelette, snails, Montbéliarde sausages, Cantal cheese, Banyuls vinegar and other French produce

Lidl
Bockwurst sausage

Mexican Grocer www.mexgrocer.co.uk
Pasilla chillies

Real Foods www.realfoods.co.uk
and **Abel & Cole** www.abelandcole.co.uk
Sea asters (aka pigs' ears)

FURTHER READING

Behr, Edward, *The Food and Wine of France: Eating and Drinking from Champagne to Provence* (Penguin 2016)

Bienassis, Loic and Jöel Robuchon, *French Regional Food* (Frances Lincoln 2014)

Bourdain, Anthony, *Anthony Bourdain's "Les Halles" Cookbook: Strategies, Recipes, and Techniques of Classic Bistro Cooking* (Bloomsbury 2004)

Child, Julia, *The Way to Cook* (Alfred A. Knopf 1989)

Conran, Caroline, *Sud De France: The Food and Cooking of the Languedoc* (Prospect Books 2012)

David, Elizabeth, *French Provincial Cooking* (Michael Joseph 1960)

David, Elizabeth, *An Omelette and a Glass of Wine* (Robert Hale & Company 1984)

Gentner, Florence, *The Monet Cookbook: Recipes from Giverney* (Prestel 2016)

Harris, Joanne and Fran Warde, *The French Kitchen: A Cookbook* (Doubleday 2002)

Olney, Richard, *Simple French Food* (Atheneum 1974)

Scotto, Elisabeth, *France, the Beautiful Cookbook* (HarperCollins 1989)

Willan, Anne, *French Regional Cooking* (William Morrow & Company 1981)

ACKNOWLEDGMENTS

Thanks to the following at Ebury Books: Joel Rickett, Managing Director, Lizzy Gray, Publishing Director, Charlotte Macdonald, Editor, and my publicist Claire Scott. Great to have been working with project editor Jinny Johnson again.

Once again too, big thanks to Portia Spooner for collating and testing the recipes and for a great deal of research.

Thanks to Alex and Emma Smith for a beautiful-looking book, and to James Murphy for the wonderful photographs. Thanks to Aya Nishimura for the attention-grabbing look of the food in the photos, to Penny Markham for the time-worn French plates, casseroles, gratin dishes and pans, and to Sarah Yorke for all the PDFs and for keeping the whole studio going. Photography days are always an enjoyable time, especially with the lunches from local delis and James and Alex's wine.

For Secret France, the TV series, thanks to Adam De Wan, Editor, who stood in as director for the late and much-missed David Pritchard, and to Arezoo Farahzad, Producer, who undertook most of the research trips, as well as giving amazing support while we were filming. As ever, I wouldn't be without the crew: Chris Topliss, Cameraman, Pete Underwood, Sound Recordist, plus Second Cameraman and Drone Operator Martin Willcocks. A special thanks to Liz Stone and Valerie Sykes for excellent research, and to all the hard-working team at Denhams, not forgetting Chris Denham himself, who organised my first camera test with David more years ago than I care to mention. Also thanks to a late arrival to the TV production team, Edit Producer Kent Upshon. Thanks to Valérie Berry for ten days of solid back-up, preparing and cooking dishes for filming in Provence, and to PA Alice Williams.

Thanks to Matthew Fort, Diana Henry, Pierre Koffmann, Rowley Leigh and Lizzie Spender for some excellent French tips.

A big thank you to my PA Viv Taylor and Jane Rees for keeping us all in touch from Padstow, and lastly the biggest thank you to my wife Sas, who came on lots of the filming trips, has always been completely supportive and is now indispensable.

INDEX

In memory of David Pritchard 1945–2019

0987654321

BBC Books, an imprint of Ebury Publishing
20 Vauxhall Bridge Road, London SW1V 2SA

BBC Books is part of the Penguin Random House
group of companies whose addresses can be found
at global.penguinrandomhouse.com

Penguin
Random House
UK

This book is published to accompany the television series entitled
Rick Stein: Secret France first broadcast on BBC Two in 2019.
Rick Stein: Secret France is a Denhams production.

Producer: David Pritchard
Director: Adam De Wan
Executive producer for Denhams: Arezoo Farahzad
Executive producer for the BBC: Ricky Cooper

First published by BBC Books in 2019
www.eburypublishing.co.uk

A CIP catalogue record for this book is available from the British Library

ISBN 9781785943881

Printed and bound by Firmengruppe APPL, aprinta druck, Wemding, Germany
Penguin Random House is committed to a sustainable future for
our business, our readers and our planet. This book is made from
Forest Stewardship Council® certified paper

MIX
Paper from
responsible sources
FSC® C018179

Commissioning editor: Lizzy Gray
Editor: Charlotte Macdonald
Home economist: Portia Spooner
Design and art direction: Smith & Gilmour
Photographer: James Murphy
Project editor: Jinny Johnson
Food stylist: Aya Nishimura
Prop stylist: Penny Markham
Illustrator: Andy Smith